Symbolic Wounds

BRUNO BETTELHEIM

SYMBOLIC

WOUNDS

Puberty Rites and

The Envious Male

New, Revised Edition

COLLIER BOOKS
NEW YORK, N.Y.

This revised Collier Books edition is published by arrangement with The Free Press of Glencoe, Inc.

Collier Books is a division of The Crowell-Collier Publishing Company

First Collier Books Edition 1962

Grateful acknowledgement is made to the following publishers for permission to reproduce quotations from published works: Allen and Unwin Ltd., The Blakiston Company, Coward-McCann, Inc., Chatto and Windus, The Clarendon Press, Edward Arnold, Ltd., Faber and Faber, Ltd., Funk and Wagnalls Co., The Hogarth Press, Imago Publishing Co., International Universities Press, Alfred A. Knopf, Inc., Liveright Publishing Company, The Macmillan Company, W. W. Norton and Co., Oxford University Press, *Psychiatry, The Psychoanalytic Review,* Routledge and Kegan Paul, Ltd., and St Martin's Press.

Library of Congress Catalog Card Number: 61–18552

Preface

IN PLANNING AND DRAFTING this book, in collecting and discussing the anthropological data, and in many other ways I was greatly helped by Ruth Marquis. By the time the manuscript was completed other interests claimed her and Kathleen Ray stepped in to edit the text for initial publication. For that arduous task I owe her much thanks.

When this new edition was planned, it offered a welcome opportunity to eliminate some of the shortcomings I had grown aware of in the intervening years, to make additions that I hoped would clarify my thesis, and to correct errors that friends and reviewers had brought to my attention. Revision also afforded a second chance to make the book a more readable one. It was fortunate for me that Mrs. Marquis was again able to help me with the new edition. Thanks to her, it was brought closer to our original plans, and enriched by what we had both learned in the meantime. A note of thanks to her here is only an inadequate expression of my gratitude.

The observations on children living at the Sonia Shankman Orthogenic School of the University of Chicago, which first aroused my interest in initiation rites, were made by several staff members, to all of whom I wish to express my appreciation.

Because I went beyond the field of my specialization and competence in this book, the advice and criticism of friends and specialists were much needed and valuable. I particularly wish to acknowledge the many helpful suggestions I received on the initial manuscript from Paul Bergmann, William Caudill, Fred Eggan, Robert Fliess, Maxwell Gitelson, Jules Henry, Morris Janowitz, Gardner Murphy, David Rapaport, Fritz Redl, Jack Seeley, Walter Weisskopf, and Fred Wyatt. They were responsible for none of the book's shortcomings (some of which they pointed out to me), and contributed a great deal to whatever merits it may have.

Those who later reviewed the book I wish to thank for their helpful criticism and for their very generous treatment of a novice in the field of anthropology. Some of their criticism I have discussed in the body of the text. But some of it I preferred to discuss here, since it deals with the overall method I used and not with any specific conclusions I arrived at.

I was accused (and rightly so if such be wrong) of "lumping all primitive peoples together"[1] and of "equating child, psychotic and primitive man."[2, 3] And it is true: I am convinced that all men share certain feelings, desires, and anxieties, that these are common not only to various preliterate tribes—as well as to children, psychotic adults, and primitive man—but to all of us. Both the practice of psychoanalysis and my work with schizophrenics, all with members of modern Western society, has convinced me, as it did many others before me, that one can and does discover the same tendencies in all men. In children and some schizophrenics they are more readily and openly visible, while in "normal" Western adults they may be carefully hidden.

Thus, far from wishing to draw parallels between primitive man (preliterate or otherwise) and schizophrenic youngsters, I tried to show how parallel are the primitive wishes of all men. The parallel is just more apparent in schizophrenic youngsters (who have radically withdrawn from adjusting to the demands made of modern Western man) and in those who were never faced with the problem of rejecting these demands, whose behavior meets the demands of their own society rather than rejects them.

We are hardly in need of proof that men stand in awe of the procreative power of women, that they wish to participate in it, and that both emotions are found readily in Western society. As a matter of fact, some poets find these emotions the source of some of the highest achievements of the Western mind,[4] and at least one literary critic has reached similar conclusions.[5] My own purpose was to show that some preliterate societies, far from being inferior to us in this respect, made the spontaneous move from the negative experience of fear to the positive experience of mastering it—by trying to make women's power their own.

This, one friend and reviewer recognized, saying: "The author, however, does not seem to me to strengthen his case as much as he might by discussing tranvestism—for instance, among the Plains Indians—as in part an escape by men from the responsibilities of the male role

Contents

TO THE MEMORY OF

Sigmund Freud

WHOSE THEORIES ON SEX AND
THE UNCONSCIOUS PERMIT A FULLER
UNDERSTANDING OF THE MIND OF MAN

with its need to fight and strut, while the new (berdache) role also of course avoids the 'labor' burden and the menstrual 'curse' imposed on women. In the modern world where this formalized escape is absent, male homosexuality may serve similar purposes; but, on the whole, men, by virtue of the very patriarchal dominance which puts them on top, must repress the extent of their longing for the simplicities and indisputable potentialities of being a woman, whereas women are much freer to express their envy of the male's equipment and roles."[6]

It is exactly because that wish is so deeply repressed in Western man, and the fear of such a wish is so great nowadays, that so many men escape into overt or unconscious homosexuality.

In brief, far from "lumping all primitive people together," I am convinced that they share with all of us certain needs and wishes that are basic to mankind. These emotions are so basic that the more varied the societies, the greater the vicissitudes they experience; in some societies they are elaborately repressed, denied, and covered up; in others they are equally elaborately transformed into social customs; or both. Again, these wishes are primitive not as belonging to primitive persons or societies, but in the literal sense of being primary, original, not derived. Thus my book does not deal with primitive man (a concept I have no use for) but with the primitive in all men (which interests me greatly).

I have no quarrel with those ethnologists and anthropologists who fear that if we overstress what is common to all men we obscure the vast differences that exist between tribes and customs that may still be very alike in externals. Theirs is a corrective position to an earlier ethnocentrism that tried to evaluate customs by the degree of their similarity to our own. Certainly psychoanalysis is dedicated to the unique ways in which each of us deals with the primitive needs and anxieties we share with all men. The disagreement, if one exists between some of my reviewers and me, is that I believe puberty rites to refer to something so primitive that all men share in it; this thesis they either disagree with or else they are simply more interested in how differently the tendency is experienced in different cultures.

In my opinion, scientific development is often a dialectic process, at least in those sciences dealing with human beings in their interactions: the overall generalizations form the thesis; the study of specific differences form the antithesis exploding the old generalizations (or the other way round). In the case of initiation rites, a series of overgeneralizations based on too little regard for detail led to a psychoanalytic thesis; those functional anthropologists who insisted that specific differences made the overall thesis invalid were a much needed antithesis. This book may then be viewed as an effort—however inadequate, perhaps even premature—to arrive at a new synthesis. If a new antithetical process then begins, it will eventually bring about a new synthesis on a higher level of understanding.

In concluding this digression into the merits or demerits of generalizations in relation to cultures, I refer the interested reader to a recent controversy about Frazer, the father of modern anthropology, which sums up the two opposing positions.[7] As long as such controversies continue, we may yet arrive at a higher synthesis.

BRUNO BETTELHEIM

Symbolic Wounds

An Ancient Riddle

PROBABLY THE FIRST INVENTIONS of the human mind, once it ceased to be occupied solely with survival, were some rudiments of religious ritual and belief. The origin and primeval form of these first creations of the human imagination will be shrouded forever in the same darkness that hides the origin of man himself, the early development of his mind, and the begining of his social structures. The beliefs and rituals of present-day preliterate peoples are only the most recent phases in a long and complex sequence, one that is unknown to us as well as to them. We cannot speak certainly of their origin by studying the characteristics they exhibit today. Still, there is hardly a more fascinating topic for speculation; our curiosity leads us to wonder what were the forms of man's first religious thoughts and rituals and what emotional needs they were meant to satisfy.

So closely interwoven are rituals and those structures that make for social cohesion that often it is hard to know where the one ends and the other begins. This is particularly true of initiation rites, to which this study is devoted.*

But whatever their origin and meaning they must arise from deep human needs, since they seem to have sprung up independently among many peoples, although in different forms. Frazer, who studied almost all rites and myths, concluded they were the "central mystery of primitive society."[1] Moreover, circumcision, which plays a prominent part in many initiation ceremonies, is one of the most widely distributed human customs. It seems that only the Indo-Germanic peoples, the Mongols, and the Finno-Ugrian-speaking peoples were entirely unacquainted with it before modern times.[2]

Even where knowledge of the operation seems to have spread by diffusion, a people, as Ashley-Montagu remarked, does not simply adopt such a practice by a sort

* When I speak of initiation, here and throughout this book, I mean initiation of the adolescent into adult life by means of specific rituals. The many other initiation ceremonies (for example, those by means of which an adult is admitted to a secret society) are outside the scope of this discussion.

of osmotic process.[3] Such a strange mutilation, found among the most primitive and the most highly civilized people, and in all continents, must reflect profound needs.

Still, I would probably not have wandered so far from my own field of interest and entered the to me alien realm of anthropology if nothing more than another discussion of initiation rites or of circumcision had been involved. I am a stranger in anthropology, and I can do no more than apologize for the kind of errors that will occur when one goes outside of one's field of specialization. What began as a short paper grew into a monograph as I found myself confronted with an issue that seemed to pose a central theoretical problem of human psychology. For reasons I will soon give, it raised the question: Under which frame of reference can human behavior best be understood, that of inner freedom and human autonomy, or that of coercion by blind instinctual forces or the insensible powers of tradition?

In many societies, especially some of the most primitive, the initiation ritual is doubly important: first as an experience that binds the group together and second as the tribe's most elaborate ceremonial. Because of this dual importance, and perhaps also because of certain strange, even awe-inspiring features, they have attracted much attention from modern social scientists and psychologists.

Though a great deal has been written about them, basically only two sets of explanations have been offered as to their nature and meaning. One of these comes from anthropology, the other from psychoanalysis. The first usually interprets the rites as a total phenomenon; the second more commonly selects a specific feature, often the practice of circumcision, and explains the rites on that basis.

Anthropological Interpretations

Anthropologists today view initiation as a *rite de passage* which introduces the young into adult society. Earlier anthropologists did not generally concern themselves with the reasons behind the use of particular means; hence they left unclarified the role of central and formidable features such as circumcision and other mutilations. Stressing the social aspects of initiation, these anthropologists tended to disregard the psychological motives that might account for the institution in general and for the needs man hopes to satisfy through particular features. But these needs, it seems to me, are either permanent or must recur in each generation; and since the rites survive, they must be at least partly gratified (unless, of course, one concludes that the rites now satisfy other needs than those they served in the past).

Many anthropologists hold that the main purpose of many ritual details is to separate the initiate from his old group and, after a period of relative isolation, to introduce him more effectively into the new group; others think that the purpose of important features is to instruct the initiate in tribal lore. Speiser, for example, although looking for a psychological explanation, sees initiation as merely an effort to speed the youngster on his road to adulthood by transmitting to him the "vital energy" of previous generations.[4] He does not tell us *why* this should be accomplished by knocking out a tooth or by circumcision or subincision.* Aware that this explanation is not enough to account for subincision, he considers it little more than a supplement of circumcision. Without raising or answering the question of why a supplement is needed and why this strange method was chosen, he tacitly admits that such questions are justified by remarking that as yet he cannot offer a better psychological explanation.[7]

According to Miller, initiation ceremonies "are intended to cut off the youth from his negligible past as if he had died and then to resurrect him into an entirely new existence as an adult."[8] He sees in initiation "a systematic ceremonial induction of adolescent youths into the full participation in social life. . . . Such practices represent efforts to rivet the youth securely to the regnant social order and are devices for the development of social cohesion."[9] This is undoubtedly true; but it does not clarify, for example, the function of mutilations inflicted regularly.

More recently functional anthropologists have paid greater attention to the social and psychological meaning of the rites. They describe the details and analyze the social aspects, but by and large they do not explain why

* Through subincision of the penis "the penile urethra is laid open from the meatus right back to the junction with the scrotum."[5] Spencer and Gillen, who reported most extensively on Australian tribes' practice of subincision, say that "it is certainly a most extraordinary practice, and one which it might be thought would be frequently attended with serious results; but none such apparently ever follow, though in their native condition the operation is performed merely with a sharp chipped piece of flint."[6]

the varied types were developed in the first place and why one device is preferred to another. Malinowski, for example, has written at some length about the function that initiation has for the society, as in the following statement:

"They present right through the vast range of their occurrence certain striking similarities. Thus the novices have to undergo a more or less protracted period of seclusion and preparation. Then comes initiation proper, in which the youth, passing through a series of ordeals, is finally submitted to an act of bodily mutilation: at the mildest, a slight incision or the knocking out of a tooth; or, more severe, circumcision; or, really cruel and dangerous, an operation such as the subincision practiced in some Australian tribes. The ordeal is usually associated with the idea of the death and rebirth of the initiated one, which is sometimes enacted in a mimetic performance. But besides the ordeal, less conspicuous and dramatic, but in reality more important, is the second main aspect of initiation: the systematic instruction of the youth in sacred myth and tradition, the gradual unveiling of tribal mysteries and the exhibition of sacred objects."[10]

The decision as to what elements of the rituals are "in reality more important" is Malinowski's; it seems to me to overstress an assumed end and to understress the means of attaining it. We are by no means certain that what the Western observer regards as means may not really be the end, and what he accepts as the end may be a more or less accidental result or elaboration of the means.

Many anthropological reports on the rites of individual tribes, particularly the more recent ones by functional anthropologists, come much closer to what may be a correct explanation. Mead, for example, feels that in initiation men try to take over the functions of women.[11] Ashley-Montagu,[12] Bateson,[13] the Berndts,[14] and others have recognized the important role played by female functions, especially menstruation and childbearing, in the emotional and ritual lives of preliterate peoples. If these interpretations were all collated and applied to the rituals of puberty, a different view of the ceremonies might emerge.

Psychoanalytic Interpretations

Certain psychoanalytic ideas on initiation and circumcision, though never accepted by the majority of anthropologists, have spread far beyond the circle of psychoanalysts and influenced the thinking of many nonprofessional persons. Psychoanalytic investigators, in contrast to anthropologists, have given almost all their attention to interpreting ceremonial details. While any discussion of initiation rites must rely heavily on anthropological field observations, the psychoanalytic theories seem to offer a more workable frame of reference for explaining the nature, origin, function—in short, the meaning—of some of the fundamental features that most interest me.

Psychoanalytic theories on circumcision and related customs among preliterate peoples have been widely discussed, repeatedly quoted, and in recent times (by non-anthropologists) more often accepted than not. If I find them in need of revision, I imply no criticism of psychoanalysis as a frame of reference or a method of investigation. On the contrary, my own efforts at understanding these rituals are based on both.

Current psychoanalytic theory about initiation rites takes, as its point of departure, castration anxiety and the Oedipal conflict. But the conclusion has been forced on me that just as in psychoanalytic practice and theory we have learned to go farther back into childhood, beyond the age of the Oedipal situation, so too for any adequate explanation of puberty rites we will have to consider much earlier emotional experiences, including the close attachment of the infant, boy or girl, to his mother; the male's ambivalance and positive feelings toward female figures; and the ambivalance of boys and girls, originating in pregenital fixations, about accepting their prescribed adult sex roles. These, it seems to me, offer a more adequate basis for understanding initiation rites than current psychoanalytic theory. According to that theory, the events comprising these ceremonies result from the fathers' jealousy of his sons, and their purpose is to create sexual (castration) anxiety and to make secure the incest taboo.

Indeed, as my study progressed, I became more and more impressed with a very different psychoanalytic premise for an understanding of the deeper meanings and functions of initiation rites: the premise that *one sex feels envy in regard to the sexual organs and functions of the other.*

Freud thought that all human beings are born with bisexual tendencies,[15] and he spoke of "the great enigma of the biological fact of the duality of the sexes." This problem, he felt, cannot be solved by psychoanalysis, though psychoanalysis reveals, in the mental lives of human beings, many reactions to what he called "this great antithesis" of the sexes.[16]

Once I began to view these rituals less in relation to castration anxiety and more to the duality of the sexes, it became ever clearer that the rites might have originated in this antithesis, might even have been attempts to resolve the sexual anxiety and envy that flow from it.

Another significant contrast belongs to puberty rites. Calling them age-grading ceremonies does not do justice to the particular age separation they mark. The antithesis between sexual maturity and immaturity must therefore be considered too. Initiation rites, with very minor exceptions, are characterized by the fact that they come at or around puberty; they are also called "puberty rites." Psychoanalysts were specially captivated by circumcision, one of its most striking features; giving most of their attention primarily to that rite, they established a direct connection between it and infant circumcision.

If they had started, instead, with the fact that initiation occurs at puberty, more note might have been taken of Freud's remark that it is not until puberty that the sharp distinction between the male and female character is established.[17] Thus the rites seem to emphasize the end of a span of life in which this distinction is not fully established, and to herald a new life period that should be free of ambivalence about the adult sex role. This tallies with the almost uniform view of anthropologists: that a main purpose of the rites is the definite separation of childhood from adulthood.

Once I began to consider these points, a complex but understandable pattern emerged into which many customs reported by anthropologists seemed to fit. Other practices, of course, do not easily adjust to such an overall pattern. This must be expected, if for no other reason than because of the long history of the rites, during which they were made to serve a variety of other functions in a variety of cultures. Still, certain basic features that on the surface seem to have nothing in common, such as subincision in Australia and the stopping up of the rectum in Africa,* can be explained on the basis of these premises.

* See pages 100, 128.

Two Views of Human Nature

One other aspect of this study of puberty rites should be mentioned. In my work with asocial children, delinquents, schizophrenics, and severe neurotics, I have come to see that types of behavior which appear as expressions of the most violent hostility, of "the id in the raw," are actually frantic efforts by the ego to regain rational control over a total personality overwhelmed by irrational instinctual forces. This is by no means a new observation —on the contrary, it is an accepted view of schizophrenia.[18]

A different perspective on human nature might emerge if this view found wider application as a heuristic hypothesis. Much that leads us to doubt man's humanity might then look like efforts—sometimes violent, desperate, and often unsuccessful—to affirm his humanity despite powerful instinctual pressure. For example, I hope to show how likely it is that certain initiation rites originate in the adolescent's attempts to master his envy of the other sex, or to adjust to the social role prescribed for his sex and give up pregenital, childish pleasures. If this effort succeeds, it permits the sexes to live together more satisfactorily. But even when such integrative efforts do not succeed, they stand for a positive purpose, in contrast to the negativism ascribed to them in current psychoanalytic theory.

I think the prevailing psychoanalytic opinion on circumcision and puberty rites represents an unbalanced view of the nature of human beings. It seems at least partly the result of viewing social institutions as expressing mainly destructive or irrational instinctual tendencies. This was perhaps necessary at the start of psychoanalysis, when entrenched denial of instinctual tendencies had to be counteracted. But it is a one-sided view and applies only part of the theoretic framework of psychoanalysis to the study of human nature. It reflects early theory concerned mainly with the id, and not the ego psychology which has lately come to stand in the center of psychoanalytic speculation. Ego and superego are not "mere" superstructures built upon the "only reality" of the id. The human personality results from the continuous interplay of all three institutions of the mind. Social phenomena must reflect not only one institution, the id (in this case the castrating father), but also the superego and, most of all, the ego. Societal institutions are indeed ego creations —the superego and id can only act upon the world through the ego.

I think that the functional anthropologist who asks what is the purpose of initiation for the well-being of society, though he may give a too-rational answer, has put the question correctly. We cannot be satisfied with an explanation that accounts solely for the destructive, sex-inhibiting, anxiety-evoking aspects of a great social institution, even if these play an important part. I am profoundly impressed with the great measure to which initiation rites seem to arise from efforts to integrate, rather than to discharge, asocial instinctual tendencies.

Our wish to think well of man has played many tricks on scientific accuracy, and this study was not begun in defense of man's dignity. But in my work with children I have learned that while little good results from an unjustly high opinion of persons and motives, much and serious damage may result from an unwarrantedly low opinion. If the latter prevails, valiant ego attempts at integration (which may be recognized in initiation rites despite some of the features so astonishing to civilized persons) may be misinterpreted as barely controlled aggression acted out. I think in our discussion of initiation and circumcision we have been far too engrossed in what looks like destruction (damage to the genitals) and have overlooked the more hidden fascination with pregnancy and birth. It may be that what has been linked narrowly and pessimistically with castration, truly a destruction of life, will come to be seen as resulting rather from the most constructive desires, those concerned with progeny, with new life.

That such views were in the air when I wrote this book may be seen from the fact that only a year later E. Neumann remarked:

"When we look for the psychological conditions that must have given rise to the initiation of adolescents, to the various secret rites, and to segregation, we find nothing of the sort in the normal male development; while the mysterious occurrence of menstruation or pregnancy and the dangerous episode of childbearing make it necessary for the inexperienced woman to be initiated by those who are informed in these matters. The monthly 'segregation' in the closed (i.e., taboo) sacral female precinct is only a logical continuation of the initiation that has occurred in this place at the first menstruation. Childbearing occurs in this same precinct, which is the natural, social, and psychological center of the female group, ruled over by the old, experienced woman."[19]

His views are based on such reasoning as:

"The earliest sacred precinct of the primordial age was probably that in which women gave birth. . . . Not only is the place of childbearing the sacral place of female life in early and primitive cultures; obviously it also stands at the center of all cults that are dedicated to the Great Goddess as the goddess of birth, fertility—and death. In Malekula, for example, the name 'birth enclosure' is given both to the fence within which women give birth and to the one surrounding the site where the male mysteries of rebirth are solemnized."[20]

It is hoped that this excursion into the far distant past and into the lives of preliterate people living today may hold something of value to the social scientist as well as the clinician, both laboring in the present and in our own complex society for the well-being of modern, civilized man. Indeed, it was while working with modern schizophrenic children that I made the observations (described in the following chapter) that aroused my interest in preliterate man and eventually led me back in my thinking to our own society.

Reopening the Case

SOME TIME AGO I observed a group of adolescent children* as they made plans that reminded me of reports I had read about primitive initiation rites. Their plans and actions were spontaneous efforts to master some of the anxieties brought on by the turmoil of puberty. Though they lived in a residential treatment institution for emotionally disturbed children,† this fact—to my mind—does not detract from the possible broader implications of their behavior.

It should also be noted that in some ways, children who live in boarding schools or institutions are living far more in a peer society, as an age group, than do children who live with their families. Here, as in the initiation societies of preliterate people, adolescent boys live with other adolescent boys, and the same for the girls, supervised by adults well attuned to the needs of such an age group. This permits the youngsters a much greater concentration on the most pressing emotional problem of their age: sexual maturity, and the fears and desires that come with it.

Reinforced by each other, and the curiosity of others, they dare to give freer vent to their fascination with how the same problems appear among their own and the other sex than they would if they were not living in something akin to an age society.

For example, without any move on the part of adults, the girls living in the institution (much more so than the boys) have spontaneously created what might be called a *passage sans rite*. Girls already menstruating are keenly aware when a pubescent girl is approaching her first menses; as for the girls not yet menstruating they both wish for and dread its onset. As soon as a girl menstruates for the first time, she is immediately taken in by the group who have passed that age mark. She is now one of the "big girls" and no longer part of the "little ones."

Most of the pubescent boys are intensely curious and also jealous of the girls' secret. The girls fan their curios-

* All around age 12, with I.Q.'s from 115 to 140, white, and of middle-class origin.
† The Sonia Shankman Orthogenic School of the University of Chicago.

ity and flaunt their secret in such a way that the nature of the mystery becomes anything but secret.

The encouragement to follow their own inclination, within reason, helps the groupings to form naturally; and the free expression of common interests cement the groups further. All this makes it easier for the children to convey their feelings to each other and to adults, to show openly their interest in menstruation and to engage in spontaneous actions.

A Spontaneous "Initiation Rite"

It all began innocuously enough with a group of these adolescent youngsters planning their adult lives. Because of the greater pressure of their emotional conflicts, they were less inhibited, quicker to act on the basis of motives that in the average child remain more carefully hidden. Their integration was well below normal for their age, and they played out their fantasies, which—partly because of their intelligence and lack of restraint—were always intense, colorful, and highly inventive.

The group consisted of two boys and two girls, all of whom could be classified as schizoid, if not schizophrenic. A third boy joined in their plans for short periods, but the first girl was the most active of the four. She had begun to menstruate, and this intensified her old sex fears, which were aggravated by a great resentment of her femininity. She and the two boys liked to act and were good at it; they lived out their pretended roles far more than any normal children would.

The second girl was somewhat further ahead toward recovery. But once she began to menstruate, a great deal of hostility was activated; most of this she directed against boys, by whom she felt persecuted.

One of the two boys had a strong feminine identification, was very anxious about it and also very afraid of women. Consciously he hated the idea of being a boy and wished he were a woman. The other boy saw himself as irresistible to (and hence persecuted by) women. He felt they were jealous of his sex, his looks, his abilities, etc.

All four children, like most adolescents, were fascinated by and afraid of growing up, of reaching sexual maturity, and of what it implied. The boys were particularly fearful. Their anxiety was mixed with an inability to wait—to ease their tension they wished they could hurry up and get it over with. Nocturnal emissions, which they occasionally had, did not seem to be proof enough of maturation. At various times, before and after the episode described, the boys confided to us their envy of girls, who at least *knew* they had grown up sexually when menstruation began. Boys, they felt, could never be so sure.

Initially it was just the first girl and the two boys who set out to plan their lives. To them, this meant becoming actors or entertainers, part of the world of night life, sexual excitement, and pleasure, as represented by Hollywood and Broadway. Then the problem arose of how to assure successful entrance to this fascinating world. The first girl had an idea: They would form a secret society that would help them to the top in spite of any resistance from adults. Her plan was that members of the group, both boys and girls, should cut themselves once every month and then mix their blood. This, she insisted, would be like a spell, ensuring success. The boys were hesitant at first, though intrigued enough to keep going. At this point the second girl joined the group. But after a time all four seemed to lose interest, and the project subsided for nearly four months.

Then the second girl—who until now had been more or less an outsider—began to menstruate. As soon as the other three learned of it, their sexual fear and excitement reached a new pitch. They reopened their talks, and the plans became more specific, the decision finally being that the boys would cut their index fingers every month and mix their blood with that of the menses. The first girl's desire that the boys should draw the blood from their genitals never went beyond intimating that it should come from "a secret place of their bodies." At this point it became necessary to interfere so that the children's plans might not lead to injury.

At both stages, the first girl spoke to her female counselor of her great resentment that only girls had to bleed regularly, while boys went free. To her this was another proof of the persecution of women in general and of herself in particular. Finally she told her counselor (in whom she saw a fellow victim of menstrual bleeding) rather proudly of her plan to make men bleed every month too, and of what power it would give all of them if they mixed their blood regularly.

The second girl, though much less active, also told us

afterward that she felt something should be done to make boys bleed as girls have to do.

Menstruation

Other schizophrenic girls show a different attitude toward menstruation. Overtly, they pretend to hide the fact that they are menstruating, considering it "disgusting" or "dirty." Nevertheless, they manage to make everyone aware of their menstrual periods, talk about little else and display their sanitary napkins conspicuously.

Others just refuse to wear sanitary napkins and manage to have their menstrual flow appear openly, as on their dresses. And these are sometimes girls who in other sexual matters are quite discreet. One twelve year old girl, though very outspoken about her wish to be a boy (often insisting she was a "he" and was to be called "he"), went to particularly great length in advertising her menses, but mainly when boys were around. Then she would scream at the top of her lungs about her "dripping period," and indeed arranged to have her menstrual fluid drip to the floor. But in this she was no different than others who harbored the same wishes, simply much more conspicuous.

Despite what in many girls seems like an open recoil from menstruation, on a deeper level the magic power they ascribe to it holds an irresistible fascination for them. If they wish boys to know that they menstruate, it is often because of the power over boys they believe it confers. On the most conscious level, it is the power to make boys uncomfortable if not plainly anxious; and this not through any deliberate act but just by a normal function of their bodies, by just being female. This seems like magic because it is their very femininity that makes the boys shudder, and not anything specific they have done to achieve such a power.

But whatever gives power is also potentially dangerous. What can make others anxious is a potentially destructive power; and if it can harm others it might also destroy its owner. The girl who experiences her menses this way has not really accepted or emotionally mastered the function, but remains partly at its mercy. She is not in control of her "sorcery," but at best a "sorcerer's apprentice" who at any moment may find herself subject to her own witchcraft.

So while some of these girls are sometimes conspicuous

in displaying their menses, other girls will delusionally pervert this function, associated with giving life, in the opposite direction, and the menstrual fluid becomes a potent poison. They are obsessionally preoccupied with the problem of how to get rid of the soiled sanitary napkin and develop elaborate rituals around its disposal; they are convinced that the menstrual discharge is so powerful that it could poison the entire population of a city.

Many normal women, even those who do not consider menstruation a "curse"—a curse being related to the supernatural and hence powerful and mysterious—regard it as something weird, and their attitude toward the menstrual discharge is ambivalent, a mixture of fascinated interest and revulsion. Fascinated by it, they cannot part with it and like some of our girls, cannot bring themselves to dispose of their soiled sanitary pads, but retain them as tokens of their secret powers. Their precautions in saving and hiding them are then as elaborate as those of our girls who devise complex rituals for discarding them.

Negative feelings in girls about femininity and menstruation combine easily with hostility toward boys, in particular toward the penis. The next step is to wish that boys, too, should bleed from their sex organs. Sometimes this wish to see boys' penes incised (as they are in circumcision or subincision) is so great that it has to become reality. And if it cannot be made real on a boy's body, it is made real on some part of the girl's own body which she comes to see as a penis.

One twelve year old schizophrenic girl felt most of the time that she despised her femininity and wished she were a boy. But at other times she believed herself to be both boy and girl at the same time. At such times she often acted out intercourse symbolically, using her index finger as an erect penis and a circular object for the vagina. But it was not her index finger in its normal condition that became her penis; it was the finger only in erect stiffness. This she called "my fingerbone" and differentiated it clearly from her finger as such. Whenever she had a fingerbone, it was a penis, and she was unable (or unwilling) to bend it at its joints. When she used the finger for other (even sexual) purposes, as when masturbating, it was just a finger, easily bent.

For many months, whenever she menstruated, she wanted to cut this fingerbone to make it bleed. Through-

out the days of her menstrual period she would obsessionally talk about and make efforts to do that. Several times,
despite the greatest watchfulness on our part she succeeded, and only our elaborate precautions prevented the
wounds from ever becoming serious. Thus she established
the close connection in her mind between menstruation
and incising a penis. She felt (and said) that she could
only accept her menstruation if fingerbones could bleed
too. Only slowly, as she began to accept herself as a girl
and could no longer view part of her body as a boy's penis,
did she give up her wish to cut the fingerbone. It was not
part of her body she wanted to see cut and bleeding, but
a boy's penis.

Ambivalence in Girls

Penis envy in girls is so well known and has been so
often described that its universality needs little more discussion. Our severely disturbed children merely go further
in its expression than normal girls. For example, we have
often seen a girl fill a balloon with water, press it to an
elongated form and hold it between her legs, spurting the
water out as if she were urinating through a penis.

One of our seven year old schizophrenic girls gave perhaps a much more primitive expression to her desire for a
penis. Several times a day she pulled at the skin of the
mons veneris and at the anterior tissues of the vulva, trying to elongate it, showing it off to others and saying:
"Look at my penis." This was not a substitute for masturbation. Though she masturbated often and freely, that was
(to her) an entirely different experience from her efforts
to make a penis and her belief that she had succeeded.

Other girls at the School have believed during each
mentrual period that a penis was growing in them and
were deeply disappointed every month when it turned out
to be false. Such delusional association of menstruation
with the penis is perhaps parallel to a conviction some
men seem to have: that they can acquire new sexual functions by bleeding from their genitals.

This hope that a penis may be acquired in and through
menstruation is an example of the positive side of ambivalence in girls. Many emotionally disturbed girls express
its negative side by considering the penis disgusting and
ugly. In certain severely disturbed girls the negative feel-

ing toward penislike organs goes much further. One such girl at the School, who could never accept being feminine, hated her clitoris, feeling it was a blemish on her body. She felt if she could eliminate it she would become wholly feminine and then be able to accept the fact.

Since she had to repress her desire for a penis, and since her clitoris, particularly when stimulated, reminded her of that desire, the result was a wish to be rid of the clitoris. This wish was so great that she had to take elaborate precautions to keep from tearing it out. The fear was not of masturbation as such, since she masturbated freely by letting water run over her vulva, pulling her pants up tightly or rubbing her legs together. But she dared not touch the clitoris with her fingers because that, she felt certain, would be an irresistible temptation to tear it out.

While this girl hated the penislike organ in herself and tried to destroy it, other females openly attack male genitals for similar reasons. Nor does the tendency occur only in schizophrenics. We have, at the School, one preadolescent boy whose central trauma was that his (nonschizophrenic) mother, while intoxicated, took scissors and snipped some skin off his penis. Such extreme signs of penis envy leading to incision are by no means as rare as one might wish to believe.

Ambivalence in Boys

A series of observations of several younger boys may be represented here by data collected from one seven and one eight year old. According to their chronological age, using standard methods, both should have been classified in the latency period. Since they were severely disturbed, however, the degree of sex repression that supposedly marks that phase of development had not taken place.

Each of these boys stated repeatedly, independently of the other and to different persons, that he felt it was "a cheat" and "a gyp" that he did not have a vagina. They made remarks such as: "She thinks she's something special because she has a vagina," or "Why can't I have a vagina?" Referring to another boy's unhappiness, one of them said, "I know why he's crying—it's because he wants a vagina." More persistent than the desire for female organs, however, was the obsessional wish to possess *both* male and female genitalia. They said, "Why can't I have both?" Disappointed in this desire, and envious of women because women, they felt, had the superior sex organs, both boys frequently expressed a wish to tear or cut out the vaginas of girls and women.

A third schizophrenic seven year old boy ritualized dramatically his desire for both male and female sex apparatus. He was able to switch almost instantly from one role to another. As a male, he sat on the toilet facing forward, freely exposing his penis; as a female, he sat hiding it, with his face to the wall. For a long time he did not urinate standing up; this would have been too profound a commitment to the male role. As a male, he freely and openly masturbated only his penis; as a female, he just as freely practiced only anal masturbation. As a boy he used his own name, as a girl he used a make-believe name; sometimes it signified himself as a girl and at other times as a clown who was simultaneously male and female.

Many of our very disturbed boys, without going quite so far, also insist that they have vaginas, refusing to accept the fact that girls have two lower body openings. They insist that the rectum and the vagina are one and that girls, like themselves, have only a single opening.

In other boys of varying ages who by and large accept their masculine role, we have often observed a hostility toward female sex characteristics just as violent as those of the boys who wish for vaginas. While these boys do not say they wish for female sex organs, they have many fantasies about cutting off and tearing out breasts and vaginas. Certain extremely disturbed boys have for months spoken of (more accurately, screamed about) little other than this consuming desire.

More benign but often just as pervasive in boys are the desire to be able to bear children and the feeling of being cheated because it cannot be done.* Such intense envy of

---

* Wolff stresses the frequency with which he observed envy of pregnancy in boys.[1] Reik reports observations of Abraham showing the lengths to which men may go in this envy. One patient, imitating menstruation, suffered so severely that every four weeks he had to go to bed for several days; a fifteen-year-old boy passed through a simulated pregnancy closely resembling a real one.[2] Recently Rangell devoted a paper to "The Interchangeability of Phallus and Female Genital." One of his patients fantasied his penis as a vagina and imagined that by inserting objects into the penis he was playing the feminine sexual role. Rangell remarks on the frequency with which boys, either in fantasy or reality, insert objects into the penis, often accompanied by masturbatory acts and fantasies of receptivity and female identification. Women, on the other hand, imagine that the

female sexuality is by no means restricted to women's primary sex appartus and functions. We have observed several boys tormented by the desire to possess female breasts. The wish to be able to nurse themselves (which they are convinced women can do) was only part of the motive. They were envious of breasts independently of lactation—that is, as sources of power and strength in themselves.

A riddle they repeatedly asked was: "What is the strongest thing in the world?" And they never failed to supply the answer: "A brassiere, because it holds two huge mountains and a milk factory." Girls never seemed interested in the riddle, but the preadolescent, emotionally disturbed boys were nearly always fascinated.

Circumcision

The wish to have a cirmumcised penis is very different from these boys' obsessive interest in female sex characteristics and functions. At the Orthogenic School, a ten year old uncircumcised boy, living with a group who had been circumcised in infancy, wanted the operation very badly.

Eventually we had to arrange for his circumcision because of adhesions. When told about it he was happy but anxious, as was to be expected. He spoke at great length about his fear of the pain of the operation. But after it was over he also admitted that he had feared the doctor would make a mistake and cut off too much or all of his penis. He told us anxiously that he thought he had heard about persons born "a girl and a boy at the same time," and how the "doctor had to cut it off" to make the person a girl. Thus he showed his great castration anxiety.

But powerful as his fears were, still more impressive were first his wish for the operation and afterward his pride in what he called his "new penis." This emotion

---

vagina is the same organ as the penis, as reflected in the statement of a female patient who said: "In the male the organ sticks out . . . in the female the same organ goes in . . ."[3] Similar ideas are frequently expressed by boys and girls at the Orthogenic School. Both have called the vagina an "inside-out penis," and the penis an "inside-out vagina." Parallel observations have been made by Ferenczi[4] and others. Many little boys, on first learning that women bear children, try to maintain that this is true only for girls and that boys are borne by their fathers.[5]

overshadowed his castration anxiety throughout. As soon as the wound was healed he displayed to everybody the penis he had always tried to hide. As soon as the bandage was taken off he declared, "I think my penis is very handsome and elegant now." With great pride he told how much better it functioned, how when urinating he could make a bigger and better stream and direct it wherever he chose. Now he fully enjoyed masturbation, which before, because of adhesions, had been partly painful. He summed up his feelings by saying, "Boy, I can do anything now." Circumcision showed him the organ's importance. The freed glans represented a newly won masculinity. Circumcision had indeed provided him with a better penis and with sexual pleasures not available before.

Similar observations were made by Nunberg during the analysis of an adult. The patient had experienced circumcision as a reassertion of his manliness in general and of the importance of the penis in particular: "The painful sensation around the glans after circumcision drew narcissistic libido to the penis. As a consequence, the patient became more aware of his genital than heretofore. The experience of circumcision increased penis consciousness as if it were a demonstration of the organ's importance."[6]

If not inhibited, boys ("normal" as well as emotionally disturbed ones) like to show off their penes with what might be called "phallic pride." Competitions to see who has the biggest or best penis become a matter of importance, including contests to prove who can urinate higher or farther. These are perhaps remnants of the phallic phase of development in which, it is claimed, the boy has "identified himself with his penis."[7] But they also indicate the desire to know who is further ahead in development, who is more manly and less childish. Exhibiting the glans freed from the foreskin is part of such efforts to assert manliness, and in this the circumcised boy is at a definite advantage: his glans always shows, and is often taken as a sign of greater masculinity.

In this respect, too, Nunberg's observations corroborate those made of our children. He says "by the circumcision the glans penis is freed . . . a new penis is born which looks like a phallus in erection with retracted foreskin."[8]

Since this book first appeared, I have had several communications from male readers telling of experiences they had as adolescents; how they spontaneously formed groups to prove to themselves and each other that they had reached sexual maturity, how without group corroboration they could not feel certain about it. If what they write me is true, and I have no reason to doubt it, then short of circumcision and subincision, many of the customs that are part of initiation rites among preliterate societies also take place spontaneously and sporadically among normal adolescents in Western society.

How some gangs intimidate new members before admission is well known. So is the custom that to pass muster, a boy must join in the group's common cohabitation with one or several girls. This, of course, resembles the custom that the newly initiated must immediately have intercourse with a woman.

As I write this, the Chicago papers report two assaults, one resulting in murder, where the two boys who committed the crimes claim that the motive was to prove their daring to a gang they wished to join. Without such a show of brutality, they claimed, the gang would not find them acceptable. This recalls those tribes where the slaying of a man is required proof of having reached male maturity.

Of these various communications I shall report only the one I was fully able to verify. In Havana, Cuba, pubertal boys about twelve years of age spontaneously formed groups which required that new members be able to retract their foreskins and project the glans (the boys were not circumcised). Those who could not do so were rejected as too young or too weak to join. If younger boys could not meet this requirement, some of the older boys taught them for about a week in a daily practice of retracting the foreskin. Often the procedure was very painful because of phimosis. But if after a week such a boy could project the glans, he was judged strong and masculine and became part of the group; if not, he was permanently excluded.*

Here, then, is a counterpart among normal Western boys to the spontaneous initiation society that sprang up among youngsters at the Orthogenic School. These normal boys voluntarily took on a painful manipulation of their genitals to prove they had reached sexual maturity, since the proof of maturity rested on showing that the glans could appear freed of its foreskin.

* I am indebted to Dr. Jerome Kavka of Chicago for this report.

Transvestism

Dressing up in bizarre costumes at Hallowe'en is part of this children's holiday throughout our society. On this day they are permitted to act out their asocial and destructive desires more freely than usual. At the Orthogenic School, children are at liberty to dress up throughout the year, and do so often. But, in line with custom, they dress up even more freely on Hallowe'en. Hence, observations made on this holiday may stand for many others throughout the year.

Our younger children, like normal children, masquerade as ghosts, witches, robbers, wild men, princes, animals, etc. Some children of all ages are too anxious to change themselves at all, or they may compromise with some token distortion of their normal appearance.

To our surprise, however, we have learned that pubertal children do not necessarily follow this pattern. If they have been with us for several years and have become able to use their relative freedom to express their desires, they seem to develop a very different pattern. Girls tend to dress up either as very masculine or sexually attractive boys or as extremely seductive women. If they disguise themselves as boys they make their desires clear by adding guns, fishing poles, swords, daggers, and other masculine implements or penislike tools and gadgets as an important part of the costume.

Boys, beginning about age eleven and even more at twelve and thirteen, like to dress as girls or women, emphasizing the breasts (only the largest pillows for padding will do). Some even dress up as women in the last stages of pregnancy. Interestingly enough, we have never seen the genuine transvestites—and we have a few among our children—dress in this way at Hallowe'en. They either do not wear costumes at all (perhaps it would hit too close to home for comfort) or they are satisfied with a single female garment or with using lipstick and rouge.

Often the boys who ordinarily display their masculinity most emphatically—boys good at sports, former delinquents who have to be restrained in their daring exploits—make the most effective appearance as women at Hallowe'en. Some of them masquerade so well that people on the street take them for girls. But the motivations are not simple. The disguise represents a desire to be, and to find out how it feels to be, a woman. But it is also an anxious and hostile caricature of women.

The important facts to note are that boys who in their latency did not dress up as girls or women begin to do so after entering puberty, and that nearly all the boys who come to feel free enough do so at least once. Furthermore, while our children often dress up, they do not let themselves go quite so far in playing the role of the other sex as during the special liberty of Hallowe'en.

These, then, are some of our observations of spontaneous, freely chosen behavior among modern disturbed children of pubertal and prepubertal age.

Challenge to Theory

My INTEREST in initiation rites began with a desire to understand the motives of the four pubertal children discussed in the last chapter. Their anxiety at our expected disapproval of their plan made us doubly eager to understand, since these were children for whose welfare we had accepted responsibility. But first, for the sake of readers who may not be acquainted with the psychoanalytic theory connecting circumcision with castration anxiety, the theory is restated.

Among the theoretical formulations of psychoanalysis may be found allusions to castration as a historical event, with circumcision as a ritual substitute for it. Thus: "Circumcision is the symbolical substitute of castration, a punishment which the primeval father dealt his sons long ago out of the fullness of his power; and whosoever accepted this symbol showed by so doing that he was ready to submit to the father's will, although it was at the cost of a painful sacrifice."[1]

Circumcision is thus cited as supporting evidence for the historical theory that would otherwise rest on shaky ground. Castration and circumcision then serve to explain both anxiety about sex and the boy's fear of and submission to the father. It is this fear that links circumcision to the Oedipus complex, one of the main theoretical constructs of psychoanalytic theory.

Freud himself seems to have felt less than certain at times about the validity of his theory. Describing how he arrived at his speculations on the primal father, he said: "When I further took into account Darwin's conjecture that men originally lived in hordes, each under the domination of a single powerful, violent and jealous male, there rose before me out of all these components the following hypothesis, or, I would rather say, vision. The father of the primal horde, since he was an unlimited despot, had seized all the women for himself. . . ."[2] Freud here implicitly recognizes that it is questionable to reconstruct prehistoric events, whether in the past of the individual or the species. He then reduces his own hypothesis to the status of a vision, though he would have preferred to think of it as a hypothesis.

Later, however, he seemed to conclude that such caution was unwarranted and stated his opinion repeatedly, and indeed apodictically. "We have conjectured," he said, "that, in the early days of the human family, castration really was performed on the growing boy by the jealous and cruel father, and that circumcision, which is so frequently an element in puberty rites, is an easily recognizable trace of it."[3]

In his last statement on psychoanalytic theory, Freud wrote, "The possibility cannot be excluded that a phylogenetic memory trace may contribute to the extraordinarily terrifying effect of the threat—a memory trace from the prehistory of the human family, when the jealous father would actually rob his son of his genitals if the latter interfered with him in rivalry for a woman. The primeval custom of circumcision, another symbolic substitute for castration, is only intelligible if it is an expression of subjection to the father's will. (Compare the puberty rites of primitive peoples.)"[4]

The reference to memory traces as a contributing factor seems to suggest that Freud was not fully convinced that the child's own experience—his parents' threats, their interference with masturbation, their disapproval of his sexual interest, or even his observing the genitalia of the other sex—were sufficient to explain the "extraordinarily terrifying" fear of castration.

It is this stipulated connection between castration anxiety and circumcision in puberty rites that makes initiation important for psychoanalytic theory; otherwise the interpretation of the rites, though interesting, would have little bearing on the central body of psychoanalytic thought.

In regard to memory traces as they supported his constructs, Freud said:

"In studying reactions to early traumata we often find to our surprise that they do not keep strictly to what the individual himself has experienced, but deviate from this in a way that would accord much better with their being reactions to genetic events and in general can be explained only through such an influence. The behavior of a neurotic child to his parents when under the influence of an Oedipus and castration complex is very rich in such reactions, which seem unreasonable in the individual and can only be understood phylogenetically, in relation to the experiences of earlier generations. . . . In fact it seems to me convincing enough to allow to venture further and assert that the archaic heritage of mankind includes not only dispositions, but also ideational contents, memory traces of the experiences of former generations."[5]

The belief in memory traces as transcending the individual's experience and as derived from a racial unconscious is particularly significant if it becomes the only way of understanding something so central but otherwise obscure as castration anxiety. If this symptom, as it now exists among neurotics, cannot be fully explained except on the basis of memory traces of actual castration by a primal father, then it becomes essential to know if that was a historical event.

What psychoanalysis actually reveals is simply that boys attach their first genital affection to those maternal adults who take care of them. They develop their first sexual rivalry against those whom they see as owners of the maternal figures. Erikson (and some other psychoanalysts) feels it is wrong to conclude, as Diderot did, that if the little boy had the power of a man he would rape his mother and murder his father. If he had such power he would not be a child and would not need to stay with his parents—in which case he might simply prefer a younger, more attractive or more available sex object.[6]

I believe that the fear of the father, including the fear seen in modern castration anxiety, can be fully explained by the small child's helpless dependence on his parents and by the scarcity of appropriate libidinal objects in the modern small family. In addition, the life spheres of father and child are usually widely separated from each other, which makes the father seem still more distant, powerful, and ominous.

The violence of the child's wishes is as yet little related to an understanding of what he can do; they are not controlled by his ego or tempered by any knowledge of what might or might not really happen, or of what others might allow him to do. This violence of his wishes comes at an age when he does not yet clearly distinguish between fantasy and reality, between wishes and their fulfillment.

That makes him afraid that his parents will retaliate in kind, and the fear is not reduced by any realistic knowledge of what action his parents might take. An unmanageable conflict is thus created between the child's dependent needs and desires and his hostile wishes against those he depends on for their satisfaction. This conflict then intensifies his hostility as it increases his fear of retaliation.

The observation of sex differences arouses other fears, often aggravated by inhibition of masturbation and by parental disapproval of sexual interests, if not actual threats; all of these lead to fear of losing the penis and thus heighten castration anxiety. The way out of this impasse is often a repression of sexual desires or of hostility, or both; there are also any number of other neurotic solutions to this, the so-called Oedipal conflict.

In a society in which threatening father figures enjoy great status because of religious precepts and sanctions, and in which sex is shrouded in secrecy, no theory of memory traces or of historic castration seems necessary to explain castration anxiety. I suggest that they result from a psychological process that projects recent emotional experiences, and views them as events that supposedly happened in the distant past. Another factor may be the wish of some psychoanalysts to see certain events in the life of the child as based on phylogeny rather than ontogeny. This supposed parallel has been carried too far in psychoanalytic theorizing, and the use of biological models in psychoanalysis in general should be re-examined. I think it likely that a deceptively pat biological model has helped to establish as fact the hypotheses of the primal horde and of circumcision as symbolic castration, and has led to other errors in psychoanalytic thinking.

After Freud

Beyond the work of Freud, the psychoanalytic references to circumcision and related topics are far too numerous to discuss in detail. I shall therefore mention only a few representative examples.

At the time of initial writing, Nunberg's was the latest comprehensive statement of psychoanalytic theories on circumcision, and it contains a penetrating and convincing analysis of a case in which the patient's reaction to circumcision was a major problem.[7]* Nunberg introduces his material by asserting the validity of the psychoanalytically forged link between circumcision and castration. He states that the "study of the puberty rites of primitives proved that circumcision represents symbolic castration, its underlying motive being prevention of incest."[8]†

But in his presentation and discussion of the patient's significant emotional experiences concerning circumcision, an entirely different interpretation suggests itself. This patient by no means viewed his own circumcision as castration inflicted by the father but experienced it rather in connection with his mother, or women. He had many dreams in which women castrated him.[9] In this connection Nunberg comments that those of his patients who were circumcised in childhood blamed their mothers for the operation, hated them, and in turn felt guilty themselves; he refers also to the many real instances of so-called "castrating," aggressive mothers.

He notes that circumcision made the patient feel that his penis had become similar to the vagina: "When I saw this gaping wound around the head of the penis, I thought that the bleeding vagina must look like that."[10] Yet in other contexts the patient experienced circumcision as a reassertion of his manliness in general and of the importance of the penis in particular.

Nunberg also suggests a connection between circumcision and birth fantasies. "When he at last accepted the idea that the child is born out of the mother, he imagined that in the hospital the child is cut out of her in a way vaguely reminding him of the circumcision. In fact, by the circumcision the glans penis is freed; it emerges like an infant from the mother's womb; in other words, after the circumcision a new penis is born which looks like a

* In his book Nunberg establishes a relationship between circumcision and bisexuality. But the patients on whom he bases his discussion are all men (even bisexuality is discussed on the basis of psychoanalytic experience with men only). The concept of bisexuality presupposes a physiological basis for the difficulties each sex encounters in accepting the sexual role. Tempting as it is to use this concept for explaining such phenomena as circumcision, I doubt the legitimacy of such explanations. They represent another example of a biological model influencing psychological speculations and leading to confusion of the frames of reference. Circumcision is due to psychological and social phenomena, not to a biological bisexuality.

† All that psychoanalytic studies of puberty rites really offer are speculations about the relation to castration and the incest taboo. No direct evidence of this relation is presented, much less "proved."

phallus in erection with retracted foreskin. . . . The initiated, the circumcised boy, is reborn without a foreskin and is thus a man."[11]

Nunberg also states that among the most significant manifestations of the castration complex are doubts about one's own sex as well as the wish to be, and the fear of being, of the other sex. He notes that dissatisfaction with one's own sex is widespread among primitive as well as among highly civilized peoples, interpreting circumcision as an expression of this dissatisfaction.[12] Yet in spite of these observations, Nunberg sums up his ananlysis by restating the official psychoanalytic theory of circumcision, referring to Freud's speculations on primeval man.

Like Nunberg, many of Freud's followers neglect their own observations and accept his theories on castration, circumcision, and initiation rites as established facts, no longer to be questioned. With the passage of years they seem to grow more and more firmly rooted, as if the validity of a theory were confirmed by repetition. The casual way in which the connection between these phenomena is considered a solved problem is illustrated by Fenichel. In the most comprehensive statement of psychoanalytic theory, he states that "initiation rites promise privileges and protections on condition of obedience and enforce this condition by symbolic castration."[13]

I do not criticize Fenichel, because the statement is only incidental in a comprehensive work. It is not so much Fenichel's own view as a faithful summary of prevailing theory.

Another psychoanalyst, Bonaparte, in an interpretation of Poe's writings, said: "This dread of the worst imaginable mutilation, the loss of the penis, . . . represents [the child's] first great fear in relation to the community and, more even than separation anxiety, determines what its future moral code will be. The danger of castration, little as it need be feared nowadays, doubtless once existed in prehistoric times. Then the father of the primal horde, originator of our earliest morals, would doubtless have thought little of killing or castrating his rebellious sons when they coveted his females."[14]

No evidence has yet been presented to show that man ever lived in an organization such as the primal horde, or that such a horde was ruled by a father who was so recognized. Even if there once was such a father, we do not know his thoughts on any matter.

To present these speculations as facts, simply because they originated with Freud, is not science but mythology. The analyst rightly feels he must have the statements of his patient to know for sure what goes on in the patient's mind; we should be at least as wary of ascribing thoughts to our primitive forebears.

Growing doubts

Returning now to our four pubertal children, it seemed clear that there were four major aspects to their spontaneous efforts at group formation. These were (1) the secrecy of the rite, (2) the boys' cutting themselves monthly in a secret part of their bodies, (3) the loss of blood by the boys and its use in parallel with menstrual blood, and (4) the conviction that this ritual would assure sexual pleasure and success in the adult world.

The more we speculated on the children's motives, the more impressed we were with the similarity between what they wished to do and certain features of the puberty rites of preliterate tribes.

One factor, even more than any details, identified the children's plan as an initiation rite: their willingness to suffer pain in order to assure entrance to an adult society which, they imagined, freely enjoyed sex. This made their enterprise functionally equivalent to an initiation rite, since anthropologists and psychoanalysts agree that pain in initiation is the price adolescents pay for the prerogatives of adulthood.

But the differences between the children's known motivations and those ascribed to preliterate people by psychoanalytic theory were also very marked. The theory asserts that circumcision at puberty is imposed by castrating father figures on their reluctant sons, with the purpose of forcing them into submission, particularly sexual submission.

Among our children, by contrast, it was the girls, not the boys, who inaugurated the plans; and it was the boys' fear of their overpowering mothers (not fathers) that seemed important in making them accept the girls' proposals.

If symoblic castration was being arranged, women were

arranging it. Moreover, the boys were receptive to the girls' ideas, and the purpose and expected result was by no means submission to parental demands. The children knew that their parents—and also we at the School who, in a way, served as parent substitutes—were opposed to their ritual and to their desire for sexual satisfaction in a promiscuous entertainment world. By means of the rite, they expected to be able to flout our adult demands— not to lose or cede the power to resist them.

Like the psychoanalytic investigators who studied puberty rites, we were at first most impressed with the part of their scheme that included bleeding from the genitals; *i.e.*, an operation resembling circumcision, if not castration. So our first efforts at understanding were made in terms of the castration complex. In this we were supported by the fact that all four children, and certainly the two boys, suffered from castration anxiety (along with many other anxieties, preoccupations and delusions). Still, we had lived with these children for several years and had studied the psychological motives underlying their behavior. On the basis of what we knew about them, it seemed certain that their project sprang up spontaneously with the onset of menstruation in the girls, and that the resulting behavior was entirely different from their ordinary methods of dealing with castration anxiety.

Thus again and again we found our understanding blocked. The elegance of the initiation theory and its general acceptance (at least by psychoanalysts) continued to tempt us to look for an explanation on that basis. But in doing so we caught ourselves neglecting some facts, distorting slightly but effectively certain facets of our knowledge of the children, and explaining events in line with theory instead of using experience to test the validity of the theory. In short, we found ourselves trying to wring understanding from theory instead of from facts.

When I began to study the anthropological literature on initiation, I found that field observations seemed to support my growing doubts about the validity of the psychoanalytic theory. Those field reports considered in relation to the children's behavior suggested new hypotheses. On the basis of these, I reviewed many other observations I had made of children (some of which are noted in the preceding chapter) and found that these types of behavior began to be more understandable.

New hypotheses

I do not attempt to establish the following hypotheses as valid, but only to show that they are just as reasonable, or more so, than current psychoanalytic theories on initiation. They need to be tested by field studies which may validate some, cause others to be discarded or radically modified.

1. Initiation rites, including circumcision, should be viewed within the context of fertility rites.
2. Initiation rites of both boys and girls may serve to promote and symbolize full acceptance of the socially prescribed sexual role.
3. One purpose of male initiation rites may be to assert that men, too, can bear children.
4. Through subincision men try to acquire sexual apparatus and functions equivalent to women's.
5. Circumcision may be an effort to prove sexual maturity or may be a mutilation instituted by women, or both.
6. The secrecy surrounding male initiation rites may serve to disguise the fact that the desired goal is not reached.
7. Female circumcision may be partly the result of men's ambivalence about female sex functions and partly a reaction to male circumcision.

No single set of theories can cover more than the essence of initiation rites, because by now they are infinitely varied in form, in content, and origin. Many ritual details are explainable only by conditions that prevail in the society they occur in. One great advantage of the accepted psychoanalytic theory is that it seems to account for all initiation rites simply, concisely, and universally. But this, it appears, is also the root of its major shortcomings. Because in order to maintain such economy and elegance, certain facts have been forced to fit the theory and others neglected.

Later, in presenting data supporting my hypotheses,* my goal is limited. The anthropological field observations are so numerous that it would take a lifetime to evaluate

---

* In which I shall not follow the above sequence because that would mean tiresome repetition of points that apply to more than one hypothesis.

them. I have found no data in the field observations or in the psychoanalytical literature to contradict my hypotheses. Where contradictions seem to exist, they are traceable not to original source material but to how it was interpreted, and these I have felt free to disregard.

At this point the question may be asked: How is one to justify basing initiation-rite theory on observations of twentieth-century schizoid or schizophrenic children—and conversely, interpreting the behavior of such children in terms of the actions of preliterate people at puberty? Indeed, such a procedure is not certainly valid, having more the character of an *argumentum ad judicium*. Therefore, although some of my next comments follow a precedent set by Freud, they should not be swallowed whole.

Freud introduced his anthropological speculations by remarking that the psychic life of the so-called savage and semisavage races "assumes a peculiar interest for us, for we can recognize in their psychic life a well-preserved, early stage of our own development." This I consider doubtful, since I do not believe that ontogeny simply repeats phylogeny. But when Freud goes on to say that "Comparison of the psychology of primitive races . . . with the psychology of the neurotic . . . will reveal numerous points of correspondence,"[15] then he refers to heuristically valid hypotheses of comparative psychology, except that I do not believe they should be restricted to neurotics, but extended to the psychology of all persons. Still, it is on the basis of his remarks that interpretations of childhood experiences have since been used freely to support speculations about primitive behavior and vice versa.

Here, one might even speculate that if preliterate peoples had personality structures as complex as those of modern man, if their defenses were as elaborate and their consciences as refined and demanding, if the dynamic interplay between ego, superego, and id were as intricate, and if their egos were as well adapted to meet and change external reality—they would have developed societies as complex as ours, although probably different. Their societies, however, have remained small and relatively ineffective in coping with the external environment. It may be that one of the reasons for this is their tendency to try to solve problems by autoplastic rather than alloplastic manipulation; that is, by altering their bodies or behavior instead of the physical environment.

Two very thoughtful reviewers took strong exception to these remarks, one called them a delusional statement, while the other felt repelled by my speculations.[16] Though I have given the matter considerable thought I see no reason to change them save to label any remarks more clearly as speculation. Still, the reader is warned that at least two scholars were convinced that I am here in error.

My reason for not heeding their criticism is that I do not claim that preliterate people cannot have as complex personalities as modern man, but only that they do not. I do not doubt their potentialities; on the contrary, my whole thesis is based on the conviction that fundamentally we are all more or less alike. It is exactly because I believe that our potentialities differ but little, that there must be some other reason why different groups of men have developed differently. Why indeed should some groups have questioned the human condition, tried to understand themselves, the world and each other, and in the process of their quest, built complex edifices, changing themselves, external nature, and their societies on the basis of greater rational understanding? Why should one group of men, over the years, small step by small step, have created modern society, modern science, and modern technology, and another group, for a similar period of time, remained relatively stationary under conditions such as those of the Australian aborigines? If this difference is not to be found in the one group's development of an ever more complex personality structure on a basis common to both, then I would like to be told what else accounts for the difference. Otherwise, we return to the belief in a basic difference of intellectual endowment between different groups of man, a belief that I hope has been relegated to those prejudices we outgrew as we developed rationally and in the complexity of our personality structure.

Since my comments were misunderstood by two separate scholars, the burden of defense rests with me. Unfortunately I can again do no better than an argument *ad judicium*, because this is an issue where knowledge is lacking, though we continue to penetrate our ignorance. For obvious reasons the following example is taken from the relationship of parent and child which looms so large in this book.

In settings more primitive than ours, sex may be less shrouded in secrecy, but everything else is more shrouded in permanent ignorance. This ignorance may take the form of uncertainty about how a child is conceived or what causes the sequence of seasons or of rain in dry countries, so important for the regeneration of plants and with it the availability of food (for without sufficient rain, the child in more primitive societies may go hungry for a year or even starve). The modern child may know much less about sex than his preliterate counterpart and much less about where his sustenance actually comes from. After all, the modern city child knows that despite the stories we read him, the farmer does not give us our food since we buy it at the supermarket for money. But by what secret manipulations his parents manage to assure a recurring supply of this money—that is a much greater unknown to him than is food gathering to the Australian aboriginal child. Thus the modern city child actually knows less, is surrounded by many more mysteries he will have to penetrate. But he knows, and here's the rub, that potentially he can know the true cause of impregnation, of how money is earned, and why the farmer is willing to sell food for money. It is this conviction—that you can know as soon as you have acquired enough knowledge—that gives such great impetus to the modern child to develop what I call a complex personality structure. No such powerful appeal to develop his ratiocination is made to the preliterate child. And since one of the secrets the child is most curious about, sex and intercourse, is no secret to him, a great stimulus to find out about secrets in general is lacking. As for the modern child, his wish to unravel it may create the desire to unravel other secrets, too. Such a desire is supported by the conviction of society (including the mass media) that through higher learning all secrets can become known. And this, particularly if the child has learned what lies behind the great secret of sex, may give him the courage to explore many others on his own.

Observations such as this one are what led me to connect complex society with complex personality structure, including complex psychological defenses, and defenses against them. They led me to assume that while in primitive society more of the basic facts are known to the child, this knowledge removes an impetus to develop a very complex personality structure. In short, I believe that primitive children could develop personalities as complex as ours, but their conditions of life give them little reason to do so.

Roheim has said without qualification that the Australian's culture is autoplastic.[17] (He did not, however, apply the concept to circumcision.) In our own society we may see a small child frustrated in his efforts to master a toy or a situation hit himself or bang his head against the floor; he does not stop to reason out if the frustration began in the external world or in his emotions. Similarly, persons in preliterate societies often act as if external reality can be met only by resignation or by doing something with or to their bodies. Further, the small child tries to become like his mother, not by adopting her way of behaving or trying to live by her values, but by wearing her clothes. In the same way some preliterate peoples tend to copy externals rather than internalize less visible characteristics. When men by subincision make themselves *resemble* women, the obvious reason is that they are trying to *be* women. Only if the data themselves rule out such an interpretation must we search for another.

Another indication of the relatively undeveloped state of the primitive's ego is that the superego seems at times extremely cruel and at other times hardly able to assert itself. How valid such comparisons may be is, of course, not established. But if the theory of comparative immaturity, of a relatively poor personality integration is correct, then the net result may be that the barriers against expression of certain tendencies are low. Thus in preliterate cultures a person might act out freely what in Western man would be taken for signs of personality disintegration; he may ritualize desires that in "normal" persons in our culture must be deeply repressed or else integrated and sublimated, that can at most be expressed only in fantasy.

I was further guided by the assumption that motivations which in "normal" persons are unconscious are often expressed openly by schizophrenic adults, and that "normal" children show behavior that in "normal" adults remains hidden. Therefore it seemed reasonable to conclude that the content of the unconscious is apt to be most visible in the behavior (and statements) of schizophrenic children. Fenichel, as a matter of fact, goes so far as to say that "in schizophrenia 'the unconscious is conscious,' "[18] and in all probability this is even truer of schizophrenic children than of schizophrenic adults.

Although psychoanalytic theory holds that the unconscious remains relatively or wholly untouched by the process of civilization, I am not convinced. Only a full study of the unconscious of preliterate peoples would permit definite opinions on the matter. What I do believe is that if persons in entirely different settings develop similar types of behavior in response to a like challenge (in this case the onset of puberty), they are motivated by similar desires; this seems the more likely if the known facts should support rather than contradict such notions. Still our children's behavior can only suggest a review of our theories on the motives of preliterates: it does not tell us what these motives are.

One cannot, for example, ignore the fact that the boys at the Orthogenic School suffered from sex fears that were probably much stronger than those of preliterate adolescents, and that this affected their motives.

The desires and motives of the boy who so warmly praised the advantages of circumcision were very different from those of the two who joined the secret society. His case does not permit unequivocal inferences, because, first, he was living among boys who had been circumcised since infancy, and, second, painful adhesions interfered with full functioning of the penis. From this we cannot draw conclusions about the emotions of boys in preliterate societies toward circumcision, if they are not suffering from adhesions. What his behavior does show is that living among circumcised men may make circumcision appear very desirable, and this condition obtains in most societies that include circumcision among their initiation rites.

As for the anthropological literature on initiation, while it supports some of my conjectures about the children's behavior, it supports them only equivocally. There is no easy parallel between the behavior of youngsters in our highly civilized twentieth-century—children who have grown up in a more or less patriarchal and sex-repressive society—and that of children reared in a society granting relatively great, often full, sexual freedom. Symptoms cannot justifiably be compared out of context, particularly when they originate in vastly different social and psychological fields. So here, too, while my experience led me to challenge the accepted interpretations of certain aspects of initiation rites, and to elaborate and qualify others, it offered mainly the stimulus to investigate further.

Some Initial Comparisons

What, then, were the points of resemblance between the study of initiation as reported by field workers and the examination of the conduct of our children?

The first point of resemblance was that through their planned secret society these four pubertal children, like the novice at initiation, tried to move themselves by a magical act once and for all out of childhood into adulthood. For the girls this required that they find ways to accept the feminine role, a task that first menstruation often suddenly and traumatically imposes on the maturing girl. To make at least this aspect of femininity—the one of most concern at the moment—more acceptable, they created a situation in which menstruation was no longer a liability of their sex alone. If this also made the boys more similar to themselves, they might seem less fearsome, less different and strange.

Other attitudes toward menstruation can also be explained in part by the search for ways of accepting the feminine role. Viewing menstruation not as something debilitating but as something that confers extraordinary magic powers may make genital sexuality more acceptable. The new power again makes men seem less enviable and dangerous and sexual intercourse with them less hazardous. All of which makes it easier for girls to give up the pregenital, pre-Oedipal strivings that Freud was the first to recognize, calling it the child's polymorphous-perverse disposition.[19]

Retaining soiled sanitary pads, etc., may represent a desire to retain proof that sexual maturity has been reached; where it results from the contrary wish to remain a child, then menstruation is viewed as disgusting.

Another point of resemblance is the woman's desire for male genitals which is seen in both initiation rites and in our children's behavior. The girl who pulled at her skin in the genital region hoped to develop a penis. She did not, however, give up either her vagina or the future ability to bear children, which she frequently acted out. Unlike the four adolescent children, she was not motivated toward greater sex maturity or adult independence. Her actions, like those of the younger boys, originated in the desire to find fulfillment in both sexes, either simultaneously or in rapid succession. She reminded me of those African girls who, at about the same age, manipulate the clitoris or labia or both so that they become enlarged and pendent (I am tempted to say) like a penis.* This distortion of the female genitals is required by tribal custom among several peoples. At present it is not imposed by men but is insisted upon by women, contrary to some widely held notions. The field reports do not suggest that the little girls conform to custom unwillingly.

The opposite of this is extirpation of the clitoris, an operation that forms part of the initiation rites of girls in several tribes. Although excision is usually performed by women and not by men, the general assumption is that the custom is forced on women by men. The desires of our little boys indeed suggest that some men would excise part of the female sex organs if not prevented. But the example of the girl who had to prevent herself from tearing off her own clitoris raises a doubt as to whether even this far-reaching mutilation may not also be reinforced in part by spontaneous desires in women.

The "initiation" ritual of our adolescents, specifically the required cutting of the boys' genitals, was originated by a girl. It remains to be seen whether the rites of preliterate people in which an analogous operation on the male genital takes place may have similar origins.

The delusional relating of menstruation to the penis, as demonstrated by one of our girls, parallels certain beliefs of Australians regarding the subincised penis. Just as this girl fantasied that in menstruation she acquired a penis, so the Australian aborigines believe that in bleeding from their penes they acquire vulvas. Though no direct connection exists, the two types of behavior seem to express parallel unconscious tendencies.

Our boys, like their preliterate counterparts, seemed to want proof as definite as menstruation that they, too, had reached sexual maturity. They may also have tried to

* Their behavior is described on pages 143–144.

lessen their anxiety about women by pleasing or submitting to them. The act by which they hoped to do this was important in itself, since it would reproduce in them something similar to menstruation; this, they may also have felt, would give them a better understanding of women's sexuality. For the boy who wished for circumcision, the circumcised penis with the now permanently freed glans may have served as well as menstruation to assure him that his sexual maturity had been attained.

Parallel to women's envy is the desire of men to possess female genitals in addition to their own. The boys who wished this so intensely were considerably younger than the adolescent boys who took part in the "initiation" plans. But the age difference may not be specially significant, since we have observed similar desires, though less frankly expressed, in adolescent boys. The egos of the two younger boys were undeveloped, and they were much more primitive in their reactions than the four adolescents. Unrelated, utterly unable to form attachments to adults or other children, they could not act purposefully or even play for any length of time. No force would have been needed to make them change their bodies and acquire vaginal-like openings. If we had not restrained them, they might well have experimented along the lines of subincision.

These boys were less concerned than the adolescents with sexual maturity and menstruation. They wished to be of both sexes; to have vaginas like—hence to *be* like—the powerful, feared, loved, and hated women. Concomitant with this desire was the powerful urge to extirpate women's sex organs. Thus the desire to possess a vagina may represent identification with women, while the wish to excise it seems to result from the hatred and anxiety generated by women and from the desire to overpower them.

The rituals of many preliterate peoples seem to represent a gratification of both these desires: Through subincision men operate on the penis so that it comes to resemble the vulva. In the so-called circumcision of girls the clitoris and sometimes the labia are excised.

Still another point of resemblance lies in the desire of males to bear children and to participate in other female functions. The boys' hostile feelings toward women's genitalia were violent and destructive, rather than constructive. The desire to bear children is more positive; it may be viewed as constructive even when expressed by boys and combined with an envy of women because they can do so. Though few boys go so far as to act out pregnancy, we have several times observed it. But the reenactment of childbirth is a very nearly universal feature of initiation rites and "pregnant" boys are to be seen at Hallowe'en.

Our children's Hallowe'en costumes suggest a final area of resemblance to initiation rites, since masquerading as a person of the other sex, or at least wearing their clothes, is part of numerous rites. Among some tribes transvestism occurs only on very special occasions. Among others, initiation customs not only permit but require it.

Transvestism seems another indication of the pervading desires of both men and women to share the sexual functions and social role of the other sex. It also seems to assure the child that with the reaching of sexual maturity not all of his desire to share the prerogatives and pleasures of the other sex must be given up once and for all. Dressing up at Hallowe'en in the clothes of the other sex seems not only to represent the wish to play the other sex's role; it is also reassurance that from time to time this will be permitted. Thus the overmasculine boys who disguise themselves so well as women can occasionally show openly the degree to which their masculine assertion is a defense against strong wishes to be feminine. The behavior of those very unintegrated children who wish to have both male and female sexual organs takes forms that are socially less acceptable. Their desires seem to reveal not only their infantile refusal to commit themselves to any definite sexual role, but their envy of anyone who can do so. Yet even their behavior has integrative connotations, to the extent that it lessens their envy and permits them to live in peace with themselves. Still their way of doing it is obviously destructive and cannot lead to higher integration.

Resolving Antitheses

Our observation of these children suggested that a view of puberty rites integrating psychoanalytic and anthropological speculations is quite possible. In our youngsters' spontaneous behavior we saw a number of parallels to initiation ceremonies, including efforts to master their envy of the other sex, to gain adult status, and so forth.

That their plans were ineffective or potentially dangerous alters nothing. Though the children were responding to irrational pressures, the solutions they arrived at seemed constructive to them. This puts them on an entirely different basis than if they had resulted from adult efforts to create sexual anxiety and reduce the children to submission.

While their behavior grew out of threatening adult attitudes (in most cases, their parents'), it was never the wish of adults that they manipulate their own genitals or those of the other sex. This desire arose while the children were living with nonthreatening adults at the Orthogenic School. Whatever the origin of their anxiety, the wish to alter their genitals was not externally imposed against their will.

All this suggests that initiation rites may not result only (or even mainly) from hostile feelings of adults toward the young; that the experience does not primarily inhibit sex enjoyment in the young or their enjoyment of the new adult role. On the contrary, as a means of enabling youth to express some of their ambivalence about growing up, it seems intended to help them accept the adult role of their sex and to succeed in living henceforth in accordance with it.

Like the spontaneous actions of the children we observed, initiation ceremonies may be meant to foster personal and social integration in a difficult transitional period of life. They should then be understood as efforts of the young, or of society, to resolve the great antitheses between child and adult and between male and female; in short, between childish desires and the role ascribed to each sex according to biology and the mores of society. Whether or not they succeed is another question.

In this sense, what psychoanalysis has viewed so far as originating mainly in the id or the unconscious, as expressing unintegrated, destructive tendencies, may be much more an expression of the ego, which is trying, through ritual, to bring order to chaotic instinctual desires and fears.

The Androcentric Veil

I hope that one further application of my remarks to psychoanalytic theory and clinical practice will be obvious.

They suggest that certain psychological phenomena have not had the attention they deserve. Particularly, penis envy in girls and castration anxiety in boys have been overemphasized, and perhaps a much deeper psychological layer in boys has been relatively neglected.

If in this book I speak mainly about the male envy of female sex functions that is because it is less often discussed and not because "penis envy" is any less common. It seems that in any society, envy of the dominant sex is the more easily observed. In societies where men play the more important role, the envy of males and with it of the penis is more readily admitted, more openly expressed and more easily recognized; the consensus is that it is desirable to be a man. This drives underground men's envy of women since it is contrary to professed mores and therefore looked upon as unnatural and immoral.

If a tribe in which this condition exists is studied by an investigator reared in a society of similar bias, the bias of the tribe and of the investigator may reinforce each other; he can easily recognize women's envy of men, but the reverse of the coin may be overlooked or distortingly minimized. We might ask if one of the reasons why boys' initiation rites are usually much more complex than girls' is that in many societies women can express their envy of men openly, while men's comparable envy can be expressed only in ritual.

Though male envy has not gone unrecognized, it has received relatively little notice in the psychoanalytic literature. To my knowledge, it was first discussed by Groddeck. Landauer referred to it in connection with his theory that it was men's disappointment at their inability to create human beings that led them to intellectual creation,[20] a theory Chadwick had expressed earlier.[21] Klein comments that "the femininity complex of men seems so much more obscure than the castration complex in women, with which it is equally important," and that the boy's identification with his mother often results in "an attitude of rivalry towards the woman, with its blending of envy and hatred; for, on account of his wish for a child, he feels himself at a disadvantage and inferior to the mother."[22] Zilboorg speaks of the "woman envy on the part of man, that is psychogenetically older and therefore more fundamental"[23] than penis envy.

More recently, Fromm referred to it,[24] and Jacobson

devoted a paper to a discussion of boys' wish to bear children, mentioning the fact that among her male patients she had "occasion to observe . . . an intense and persistent envy of female reproductive ability—an envy which is often disguised by a seemingly normal masculinity."[25] Psychologists who follow Jung are familiar with the importance of the mother archetype (the Great Mother) and its consequences for male desires and anxieties, a point of view more recently presented by Neumann.[26] But neither these nor, to my knowledge, other authors have investigated the relation between mother figures and adolescent circumcision; between initiation rites and the youngsters' feelings about their own and the other sex; or about the need to accept the sexual role prescribed by society.

It is well known, of course, that castration anxiety in boys results from fear not only of father but also of mother figures. I hope that the present contribution to the theory of castration anxiety will be a greater emphasis on the influence of women in circumcision and other features of initiation rites (seen directly because women wanted circumcision to take place, and indirectly through the boy's identification with his mother) and a recognition that it is by no means certain that circumcision originated with the father figures.

The interpretation of initiation rites presented here emphasizes in individual psychology and in certain social institutions the importance of pre-Oedipal experiences, particularly insecurity about and dissatisfaction of *both* boys and girls with their own sex, and their envy of the other sex. Were we to recognize the importance of such tendencies, and of the effect of maternal figures in creating a desire for female sex functions, and also castration anxiety in the male, it might lead us to reinterpret certain of our social institutions and clinical observations.

The need for such reinterpretations has been recognized and commented on in the literature. Zilboorg felt that the true bio- and psycho-sociological role of woman has not been fully understood by psychoanalysis; that while Freud was aware of the problem in most of his studies, he was hampered by his masculine bias.[27] He adds, "There is no doubt that further and deeper studies of man's psyche will yield a great deal of enlightening data, as soon as one learns to discount the androcentric veil which has heretofore covered a number of important psychological data,"[28] and, "When it is resolved not to overlook how much feminine there is in the masculine attributes of that which was heretofore marked as most primary and unquestionably most masculine, and when the fundamental envy with which man treats woman . . . is borne in mind, then I am certain that clinical observations will become enriched with new material which heretofore was obscured by androcentric bias."[29]

I hope that this study may lessen the male-centering propensity and shed new light on the psycho-sociological role of woman; that it may indicate how much more that is feminine exists in men than is generally believed, and how greatly woman's influence and strivings have affected social institutions which we still explain on a purely masculine basis. Though I have chosen for more detailed analysis only the relatively narrow area of puberty rites, it should be remembered that similar factors lie behind many other aspects of human behavior and our social institutions.

The Blinders of Narcissism

TWO MAJOR FACTORS underlie what I believe to be a too narrow interpretation of initiation rites and especially of circumcision. The fact that these rituals take place in a setting far removed from our own seems to be largely responsible for both.

The first factor is a readiness (because of this alien atmosphere) to view the rites within a narrow if not sterile conceptualization, once a plausible explanation has been offered. The reduction of complex rituals to such simple terms would never be accepted for our own culture. The common anthropological interpretation of initiation rites —that they are primarily if not entirely *rites de passage* —seems an example of a valid but too narrow conceptualization. It may, for instance, account for the relative neglect of such features as the circumcision or excision of girls.

The second factor is a tendency to deny the alien by bringing to the study more or less fixed ideas, derived from our own culture, of the probable motives and emotional results of action.

I believe that the prevailing psychoanalytic interpretation of initiation was influenced by both these factors. As a result, psychoanalytic theory has been mistaken for, or been allowed to distort, fact. This is primarily a problem in the psychology and sociology of knowledge—that is, any event may be experienced and its meaning understood in vastly different ways in different societies.

The Sociology of Theories

Kris has stressed the threefold significance of psychoanalysis: as therapy, as psychological theory, and as a new and unique method of observing human behavior.[1] It is to the method of observation, he pointed out, that we owe most of the clinical hypotheses on which psychoanalysis rests.[2]

Freud's new method of observing himself and his patients developed earlier than therapy, and both observation and therapy were needed before a theoretical system could emerge. The publication of true psychoanalytic material began with Freud's observations of hysterical patients and his analyses of his own dreams and those of persons who had been treated in analysis. The theoretical papers on metapsychology crowned all his previous work.

These phases of growth may be seen in all sciences. New methods of observing and interpreting come first. These lead to the development of new systems of thought by bringing into meaningful order many familiar facts that were previously neglected, viewed in isolation, or simply misinterpreted. The next stage is more systematic observations and, finally, a theoretical system.

At the same time, the history of science provides many examples in which a theoretical system, once developed, comes to impinge on the quality of observations. Data that fits the system may be overstressed, while others that are equally valid but contradictory to theory are ignored. The result is a literal distortion of observations to make them conform to the established system. Then the system becomes more and more sterile and eventually may block instead of help us to understand. Theoretical systems, therefore, may be said to be useful only so long as they remain open to constant modification in the light of new and careful observations.

The early rejection of psychoanalysis is only one of many examples in which the understanding of data provided by a new method of observation and interpretation was blocked by an ossified theoretical system. Freud himself was fully aware of this, long before he suffered from the rejection of his own discoveries because of it. Praising Charcot in one of his earliest papers, he says: "Charcot never tired of defending the claims of the purely clinical task of seeing and classifying phenomena, as against the encroachments of theoretical medicine. One day a small group of foreign students . . . annoyed him by raising objections to his clinical innovations. 'That cannot possibly be,' one of us interrupted him, 'that contradicts the theory of Young-Helmholtz.' He did not reply, 'So much the worse for the theory, clinical facts rank first,' and so forth. But he did say—leaving us deeply impressed, 'La théorie, c'est bon, mais ça n'empêche pas d'exister.' "[3] [Theory is fine, but it does not prevent (facts) from existing.]

To date, only an occasional psychoanalytic paper indicates that theory may be encroaching on the evaluation of observations. On the whole, the first aspect of psycho-analysis—its function as therapy—is an adequate safe-guard. The patient's productions in treatment allow the psychoanalyst to observe critically and afresh, without hindrance by convictions based on theory. Even if he should now and then be guided by theory instead of by spontaneous "sympathy of the unconscious," the free as-sociations of the patient, if not interferred with, will soon correct him.

Nunberg's book on circumcision[4] reveals the vitality of direct psychoanalytic observation of patients, but it also shows signs of encroachment by theory on how observa-tions are interpreted. No bias entered into Nunberg's analysis of the case on which his book is mainly based. The feelings of the patient that ran counter to psycho-analytic theory were recorded and discussed with great insight. But in his speculative reasoning about the history of mankind, Nunberg failed to do justice to his own case material, because he accepted the link between circumci-sion and castration by the father as proved.

The danger of a theoretical system's infringing on its own method of observation is therefore present in psycho-analytic theory, and most particularly so when theory is applied to such areas as sociology and anthropology. There it cannot be checked against fact by free association or the interpretation of dreams, and the observer may work in settings with which he lacks a quick and natural em-pathy. It is always tempting to cover up an absence of spontaneous observation by theorizing. If the investiga-tor brings to the field strong convictions on the universal validity of certain theoretical speculations, he may take theory for fact. When this happens, he may treat observa-tions as if they were facts of a lower order, acceptable only if they fit the theory or if he may so interpret them that they seem to fit.

In any subject on which Freud expressed himself strongly, the danger of distortion is increased. Freud has so often proved to be right and his critics wrong that there is an understandable reluctance to disagree with his inter-pretations. This is particularly true of any phenomenon connected with so central a concept of his system as cas-tration anxiety. Still, Freud's excursions into sociology and anthropology, though full of brilliant insights, occasionally fall short of scientific accuracy. Schmidl has discussed Freud's tendency, in his sociological and anthropological treatises, to neglect important parts of the literature or to emphasize only those findings that support his theories. He also offers a plausible hypothesis as to why Freud did so little justice to the sociological literature and what motivated him in the first place to deal with sociological and anthropological problems.[5]

A related distorting factor (to which I shall refer only briefly) also influences the psychoanalytic interpretation of historical and social phenomena. This is the failure to distinguish between psychoanalytic fact and historical fact. For example, when the son, on the basis of his neurosis, fears that his father may castrate him, the father becomes a castrating father—but this is so only in the mind of his son. In reality, the son's anxiety tells us much about himself but only little about his father, who may very well be a kind man, as was Freud's friend, the father of "little Hans."[6] If in reporting such a case no clear distinction is made between the two kinds of "facts," the reader may infer that the child's reactions to his parent present a true picture of the parent or of his intentions. I believe that in interpreting puberty rites and circumcision we too have failed to separate the fantasies of patients from historical reality.*

Bias in the Observer

The way in which an event is experienced, even more than its objective content, may be important for its psychological consequences. Emotional reaction to an event depends a great deal on how the person has been prepared for it, on the anticipations he brings to it, on his *a priori* expectations. Therefore if we wish to understand how the adolescent boy in preliterate society experiences circumcision, we must know with what attitudes he approached it. Since circumcision is said to activate castration anxiety, we should know whether these boys are conditioned to look forward to initiation as an experience creating such anxiety. The question to be asked is: Do the boys really experience fear about sexual matters? (Anxiety in anticipation of surgery as surgery I set aside for the moment.)

When it comes to initiation and circumcision, the psy-

* This book may not be entirely free of such errors.

choanalyst or the psychoanalytically oriented anthropologist is likely to be a biased observer. The psychoanalyst has observed patient after patient in whom ravaging castration anxiety originated in father figures who were experienced as overpowering. When he is confronted in reality with father figures who circumcise their adolescent sons, he may be ill equipped to view this as anything but a source of deep castration anxiety for boys. But these adolescents knew a very different childhood from that of the analyst's patients. They may therefore have experienced sex in a very different way.

In discussing the castration complex Freud wrote: "Another element of that stage is invariably, I believe, a masturbatory stimulation of the genitals, the masturbation of early childhood, the more or less violent suppression of which by the persons in charge of the child sets the castration complex in action."[7] But what activates the castration complex in societies where no such suppression takes place? Is a "castration complex" that results from the open observance of sexual intercourse, or of the visible anatomical sex differences, really the same as the castration complex we see in neurotics who are kept from freely observing sex differences and activities, who learned that everything pertaining to sex was embarrassing to their parents, and whose sex activities were forcefully interfered with by their sex-anxious parents? If sex freedom for children exists in one society and sex inhibition in another, what can be the content of a castration complex that supposedly exists in both?

If, indeed, the purpose of initiation rites is to enforce the incest taboo, they occur much too late in the child's life. Among the tribes that have the most elaborate rites, children begin to have sexual intercourse at an early age,[8] long before the ceremonies take place. Also, a rite that is immediately followed by indiscriminate cohabitation with mothers and mother substitutes,[9] among others, cannot be said to be successful in enforcing the incest taboo.

Their Mores and Ours

Unfortunately, we have detailed description of Australian native sex behavior only for Western Arnhem Land. To my knowledge, only the Berndts have written a book-length report devoted entirely to the subject. Their report, however, demonstrates convincingly the absence of repressions that lead to castration anxiety. Although the Berndt's point of departure is different from mine, they too stress that ideas derived from another society are misleading if we wish to understand what sex means to persons in preliterate cultures.[10]

Among the Australian aborigines, whose society is one of the most primitive known to us and whose initiation rites are very elaborate, sexual behavior is not a topic veiled in deliberate obscurity or virtually ignored by the community. Except in the presence of certain tabooed relatives, the physical relations between men and women are spoken of freely, without embarrassment and with obvious pleasure, even in front of children. From an early age, native children are familiar with copulation. Sex is considered a normal, natural, and most important factor in human life. There is no attempt to keep anything about it secret from young persons.[11]

The Berndts describe how children are allowed to indulge sexual desires without criticism. They may be invited by a mother, older brother or sister, or some other person to have sexual intercourse with an adult or a child of the same age standing nearby. Their sexual organs may be played with or their sexual potentialities discussed at length and in detail in their hearing by older persons.[12] At an early age they learn of the sexual act by direct observation, and they imitate adult sexual activities among themselves, publicly when they are very young and somewhat more privately when they become older and more self-conscious. With increasing age the child's sexual behavior, though remaining as free, comes to resemble adult sexual activity more closely.

Kaberry, Ashley-Montagu, and indeed most writers on Australian ethnography have commented on the general absence of threatening parental attitudes in the education of Australian aboriginal children. The aborigines accept the behavior of their children and treat them with exceptional kindness, affection, and consideration. Childhood is on the whole a happy period.[13, 14] In these tribes, therefore, children do not undergo the experiences that create castration anxiety in Western culture. Not only is the child treated with love and tolerance but, what counts most in terms of castration anxiety, his instinctual desires are satisfied, not repressed.

Unlike the child in the American small family, the Australian aboriginal infant is not presented with a very limited number of libidinal choices, nor does the mother play the special role in child-rearing that is reserved for her in our society. From an early age, aboriginal children know about and understand the marriage classes. The boy knows almost from infancy that while he cannot marry his mother, there are other females who are specially suited and available as wives for him. The emotional closeness of the modern Western family, with its restrictions concerning cleanliness, movement, noise, and touch —all of which set the stage for castration anxiety—are absent.

Just as the Australian deities are less fear-inspiring than the God of Christianity and Judaism (though that image is becoming less threatening in Western culture), so also the Australian fathers appear less threatening to their sons.* Durkheim thinks that most preliterate people do not experience their deities as chiefly vengeful or threatening.[16] Anthropological evidence suggests that parent-child relations are similarly more direct, comprehensible, intimate, and less demanding among the Australian aborigines than in our culture.

Some reviewers have correctly pointed out that it is nevertheless conceivable that some preliterate societies use circumcision in the sense of symbolic castration.[17] This may certainly be so, although the evidence has escaped my attention despite a careful scrutiny of the literature. But even if it were, we would still have to ask: What were the psychological origins of the custom, and what connotations were attached to it only afterward? That circumcision, even where it is desired, can still arouse castration anxiety, I had already noted (see p. 32). Thus my intention was not to deny that castration anxiety is con-

---

*Freud has amply discussed the reasons why the God of the Old Testament is particularly apt to cause anxiety in the believer. I may add that He is much more fear-evoking than even the most threatening deities of preliterate peoples, because of His complex, if not contradictory, nature, and because He is less anthropomorphic and therefore less possible to conceptualize—His followers are not even permitted to form an image of Him. This extremely threatening quality of the God of the Old Testament has been discussed imaginatively and impressively in the first chapters of a new book by Jung.[15]

nected with circumcision, but to suggest that it is only incidental to other psychological desires.* Which merely raises again the question of what forms the essence of castration anxiety. If castration anxiety means the fear of losing sexual pleasure and potency, it certainly does not mean an experience that brings exactly the opposite, namely satisfying sexual relations, and with it pleasures not available before circumcision.

A symbolic castration that is not experienced as such is no symbolic castration for the person experiencing it. It may still be that for the person inflicting it, but from what field observers report, those who inflict circumcision on boys are not motivated by anger or envy, or the wish to create fear in the boys.

Still, my criticism of psychoanalytic theory would not be invalidated if in some instances that theory turned out to be valid; on the contrary, one of my main quarrels with explaining circumcision as symbolic castration is its claim of universality and its neglect of contrary evidence. If in my efforts to debunk it I have fallen into the error of making too sweeping generalizations, I am grateful for the chance to correct myself.

Relevance of Social Structure

The psychoanalytic image of the threatening father does not seem to fit the casual organization of primitive society either. For survival, these small groups depend on the contribution of every person to food gathering and other tribal activities. They are too little organized in inferior and superior classes to be able to afford huge ceremonies organized for the advantage of one subgroup alone.

Westerners once believed that these tribes were ruled autocratically by the elders who imposed an iron rule on the young. But it was in nineteenth-century European so-

---

* That the Tiv of Nigeria use the same term for circumcision and the castration of animals proves only that the two are connected in present-day linguistic practice; it does not prove that they had the same origin, since circumcision occurs in societies such as in Australia which neither breed nor castrate animals. That circumcision is the older of the two practices even among the Tiv is suggested by the fact that the term "ichôngo," used for both circumcision and castration, comes from the verb "tsôngo," which means to circumcise.18 Thus circumcision was not derived from castration, but the other way round; once castration began to be practiced, the older word for circumcision was used to name both.

ciety that the boy chafed under the control of the distant, sex-forbidding, and omnipotent father. In many preliterate societies there is no such gap, no alienation between father and son, between old and young. The Australian headman is no boss, no powerful father, nor in any sense a chief—indeed, there exists nothing like the office of chieftain among the Australians. The headman has no power beyond the respect he commands.[19]

This raises the question of what is meant by one group's social ascendancy over others in a given society. Who rules, for example, in a capitalist society? The nominal owners of the largest sums of capital, or the owners of the means of production? Or are the true rulers the adminstrators of large enterprises and not the owners of the shares? And what about the political rulers who may control both administrators and capitalists? Fortunately this complex question need not be answered here.

The psychoanalyst chooses other characteristics than those the economist or political scientist looks for in deciding who wields power. It may be hard to identify the ruling group, but it is easier to recognize the subordinate. Its members seem to depend for satisfaction of their instinctual desires on the permission or sufferance of their superiors. The superiors impose limitations on the id, set up examples for superego formation, decree what activities are acceptable sublimations, and so forth. This seems most clearly demonstrated in the small subsociety of the modern family. There the parents, while enjoying instinctual gratifications themselves, have the power to deprive the child of them. Often parents impose not only their own superego demands, but even more rigid standards than they themselves obey.

If a similar analysis is applied to many preliterate societies, however, the superior status of the elders becomes even more doubtful. Studies such as those of Kaberry and the Berndts indicate that Australian aboriginal children are at least as free as adults to gratify oral, sexual, and kinesthetic desires and to discharge their aggressive tendencies.[20, 21] Superego demands imposed on them in the form of social mores are in some tribes less stringent than those the parents obey.

It may be that adolescents in preliterate societies could have resisted initiation rites if they had wanted to. More accustomed to meeting adult tasks than adolescents in our society, they may have felt less dependent on or over-awed by adults. Anthropologists have indeed reported cases of youngsters' avoidance of initiation,[22] although this is the exception. Nowadays, those who wish to certainly can; but again only rarely do they do so.

Among some tribes of South Africa, initiation can only take place at the boy's own request, indicating that the choice rests entirely with him. If he is timid, retiring, or intellectually immature, he may never make the request. Though his father may hint that "it would be a good year for the ceremony," he refrains from suggesting that he wants the boy initiated.[23] Among other tribes where the first request for initiation also comes from the boy himself, he may begin the ceremony but then refuse to go on to circumcision. He is not coerced, and the ceremony must wait until he has gathered the necessary courage.[24]

The avoidance of initiation, where it occurs, is usually explained as a result of the disintegrating influence of contacts with missionaries and Western culture. So far as I am aware, however, there is no evidence that the avoidance of initiation did not occur as frequently before there were anthropologists to observe it. Perhaps the insistence that tribal law breaks down only as a result of cross-cultural influences is another example of field observations that are distorted by preconceived theoretical notions. Observers, believing in the perfect integration of remote preliterate societies, interpret deviations from the norm in accord with this idea; in reality, deviations may have occurred throughout history.

In this case, to place the blame on outside influence seems particularly dubious. For at the same time, among the same people and subject to the same outside forces, circumcision in Africa[25] and circumcision and subincision in Australia[26] are actually spreading, not decreasing. White influence reduces the influence of the tribal elders and this might, by itself, explain how some boys come to evade the ritual surgery. But the same white influence leads to the diffusion of circumcision. "Circumcision was opposed by the chiefs, but since the waning of their power under European influence their opposition has not prevented the spread of the custom."[27] Circumcision in this case clearly occurs because of the people's desire for it, not because of pressure from above.

Initiation as a Learning Experience

Because many puberty rites include both circumcision and the teaching of tribal lore, circumcision is interpreted as ensuring obedience to tribal precepts through the threat of castration. This explanation seems to represent *post hoc, ergo propter hoc* reasoning, making causal connections where no causal relations exist. Moreover, such an interpretation cannot cover all initiation rites, not even all that include circumcision, because in many tribes no explicit teaching takes place.

There is even reason to doubt that learning or teaching, whether in regard to the incest taboo or to tribal lore, is an intrinsic feature of initiation. From his comparative study of tribal initiation, Loeb found four essential elements in the rites. He does not include the teaching of precepts among them.[28]

In reading anthropological accounts, one is struck in many cases with how little, or what insignificant, teaching and learning actually occurs (unless one considers the acting out of instinctual tendencies as chiefly a learning experience).

At least a few field workers have concluded that the teaching occurs more in the minds of white observers than in the experience of those who take part in the rituals. Firth, for example, observed: "But of explicit instruction in tribal lore and manners there is usually, I think, less than is imagined, and what is given is by no means a primary feature . . . the insistence on the educative aspect of initiation comes, I fancy, from the attempt to justify rites which on first observation were described as being cruel, barbarous, degraded, and meriting abolition. When it was learnt, as in Australia, that moral and religious instruction was imparted at this time, this was grasped as an argument in favour, and sometimes exaggerated."[29]

This suggests that to view initiation rites as an educational (or superego-enforcing) experience may be a defensive reaction by which observers protect themselves against an experience that evokes quite a bit of anxiety.

I believe that deep emotional needs of both initiators and initiates, not the desire to teach and to learn, find some degree of satisfaction in initiation rites. But even if we accept for the moment the theory that an important lesson is taught, it does not follow that the experience is therefore entirely progressive or entirely inhibiting.

Among anthropologists, initiation rites are considered predominantly progressive phenomena. To the psychoanalyst, they can as easily be considered either regressive or id-motivated. Probably they are all of this. Some parts of the rituals, such as learning tribal customs, may have mainly progressive meanings and accord with ego and superego strivings. Others, such as subincision, may be the result of a "regressive" breaking through of pregenital desires and serve mainly to satisfy id strivings. Still others may be both at once.

If, as I believe, man's envy of the other sex is a major factor, the participant may well act out such "regressive" tendencies; but where the ceremonies result in a better adjustment to his own sex role, this constitutes an integrative, progressive aspect. This explanation in terms of motivation and function, if valid, suggests that attempts to explain the rites on a unilateral basis are again too narrow.

Almost any central institution of society, while it may serve the needs or desires of one sex more than the other, must to some degree satisfy certain needs of the other sex in order to survive permanently. Those satisfactions need not be primary or basic, but may be the consequence of custom. For example, certain passive desires may be activated in women who begin to live in a patriarchal society. But once aroused, they need to be satisfied. That such a society frustrates many of women's active desires goes without saying. Still, it could not have continued to do so had it not also met some of women's passive wishes.

An institution such as adolescent circumcision may well satisfy the hostile desires of a few (elders or women), but it must also satisfy certain needs of many more. The adolescent's masochism, or his wish to identify with women or with adult men, may be among them. Obviously an institution may serve the constructive desires of one group and the destructive desires of another; may serve the ego tendencies of some persons, the id desires of others, and the superego demands of a third group; may serve the conscious needs of one group and the unconscious, repressed needs of another.

It seems to me that examination of any human institution must begin with the *a priori* assumption that in some way it serves all parts of the society. Only after this assumption has been proven false is it safe to conclude that the institution benefits only one segment. The idea that both male and female initiation ceremonies (rituals world-wide in extent and going back many generations in time) have to do mainly or only with the interests of males, or of the small group of male elders, seems to violate this premise.

Yet much as anthropological and psychoanalytic interpretations of initiation rites differ, both agree that the purpose is to enforce what might be called superego demands. The question remains of what id and ego reactions are evoked.

Let us consider first those who do the initiating. Psychoanalytic theory gives full recognition to the instinctual desires of the older men in shaping the rituals, perhaps overestimating their importance. In assuring their own sexual ascendency, the elders combine hostility and superego strivings, the first by inhibiting their sons as potential sexual rivals, the second by teaching of tribal lore, assuring obedience to tradition. The actions of the elders are thus at the same time under the influence of both institutions of the mind: id and superego; indeed, they must be, since these men act as human beings, and human beings can never at any one time be motivated by only a single institution.

But what about those who are initiated? What are the positive appeals to their instincts in ceremonies that supposedly make such strong demands on their superegos or on their ability to integrate experiences? According to some students, these lie in the fact that the youngsters gain sexual freedom through initiation. But among the peoples who have developed the most elaborate initiation rites, children enjoy such freedom all their lives, and the rites can add nothing in this respect.

An analysis of the rituals makes it doubtful that only superego demands that are not equally id-motivated in both initiator and initiate are created or met in the young. There seems little reason to conclude that two sets of motivations—one in those who initiate and an entirely different one in those they initiate—are at work in a ritual that so successfully binds people together; psychoanalytic evidence suggests that the opposite is more probable.*

Even the simplest anthropological explanation of the rites as a learning experience presupposes cooperation. But psychological investigations have shown convincingly that learning is only effective and lasting if the learner cooperates for his own motives. What is difficult and frustrating can only be surmounted by strong positive motivation. It may simply be a desire to master the content, or to pacify the superego and ego (which tell the student that the experience is necessary, despite id resistance), or to please a parent or teacher, or to gain status, etc. When the student is forced to learn against his resistance, the results may be diametrically opposite to the teacher's intentions.

In our highly organized society, in which the feelings and doings of adults and children are widely separated, it is true that teachers often teach children who are reluctant to learn. But even here the most successful teaching takes place when teacher and student are moved by the parallel desire to transmit and receive, or even better, to share a common experience. These successful teaching experiences have positive connotations to both teacher and learner, and offer id, ego, and superego satisfactions to both at the same time. The most successful teaching of all occurs when both teacher and student are urged on by a similar, often unconscious, desire to master a common problem.

Psychoanalysis has also shown that parental efforts to impose cleanliness (for instance) will lead to very different results in learning and personality formation, depending on what the child brings to it in terms of expectations, past experience, etc.; whether he cooperates to please a loved parent or whether he refuses to defy a hated one. Precepts that are forcefully imposed by elders on the relatively helpless infant may lead to a host of different learnings and results—ranging from utter submission to

* Freud, in discussing the ritual defloration of girls, says that "Primitive custom appears to accord some recognition to the existence of the early sexual wish [of the girls] by assigning the duty of defloration to an elder, a priest, or a holy man, that is, to a father-substitute."[30] Thus he recognizes the possibility that such rituals are id-motivated in the adolescent girl, that this rite may be as much desired by the girls as by those who perform it.

total resistance, not to speak of an immense variety of sublimations and reaction formations.

In view of this it is unlikely that a series of supposedly traumatic experiences to which a number of adolescents are subjected against their wishes will lead to the uniform results desired by their elders. If the single result of the supposed trauma of circumcision is that the boys come to fear and obey tribal elders and to avoid incest, we might reasonably expect that toilet training should cause all children to become identically trained and compulsively clean. The more logical conclusion is that externally imposed ritual traumata should bring at least as varied results in primitive youngsters as externally imposed habits of cleanliness brings in our children. Probably the results would be even more varied, since initiation takes place when the child is older.

If, on the other hand, initiation is not entirely adult-imposed, if it partly satisfies important strivings of adolescents, then we can understand how the shared experience might produce similar results. In modern society, adolescents beset by common instinctual strivings try to be like one another, often in defiance of adults. Though comparisons between primitive society and our own are more suggestive than convincing, they may still serve to make a point that seems valid and significant for both.

Individuals seem to react dissimilarly to outside-imposed control of instinctual tendencies (as in toilet training); but when they react spontaneously and as a group to the problem of finding instinctual satisfaction, then individual development seems to be strikingly similar. If initiation were forcibly imposed on the adolescents, it would not lead to uniform consequences; if, on the other hand, it was even partially desired by both initiates and initiators, if it was a response to essentially similar strivings of the young, then the results might be relatively uniform.

Initiates, and possibly the initiators too, may feel basically ambivalent about specific rituals such as circumcision. Social pressure and approval may then lead to the more or less full satisfaction of one part of the ambivalent desire, and the token satisfaction, suppression, integration, or sublimation of the other.

To use again the example of teaching cleanliness: The human infant seems to have little interest in becoming clean. His ambivalence about toilet training results from outside influences—that is, the wish to please the parent is placed in opposition to the child's own natural inclinations. But in initiation, I believe, the ambivalence is inherently the adolescent's. He himself wishes to be grown up and also to be a child (to retain his own sex and to enjoy prerogatives of the other sex, etc.). But he also wishes to free himself of this inner ambivalence. In addition, social custom tells him which of its aspects he may satisfy and how he may deal with the others. Because adult demands and the youngster's inner wishes thus unfold in somewhat parallel fashion, the result may be more or less uniform for the group.

Considering these everyday observations on learning situations, perhaps we come to initiation rites with an extraneous frame of reference when we assume that an unwilling learner meets an overpowering, threatening, inimical teacher. This seems particularly misleading in the case of preliterate societies where the interests and activities of child and adult are so little differentiated.

In Hopes of Pleasure

In the face of so much negative evidence, why should belief in the menacing (castrating) primitive father have found such widespread acceptance in the psychoanalytic literature? A clue may again be provided by Freud who, referring to it specifically as "One of the Difficulties of Psychoanalysis," speaks of how we resist realizations that endanger our self-love.[31] The theory of evolution, while challenging our self-esteem by showing us our animal origins, flatters our narcissism even more, since it makes us the crown of biological development. Perhaps some of our anthropological speculations have been influenced by the same narcissism. It could be very painful to realize that, despite his other advances, modern man inspires more fear in his children than parents in preliterate society, and that his God is more punitive than some of the primitive deities.

It might also distress the psychoanalyst to realize that some of the theoretical constructs basic to his work with modern neurotics—constructs that he had to develop against the resistance of society and of a superego that wished to deny the existence of the unconscious—have only limited applicability. Narcissism, more than logic, may thus have led us to the conclusion that something so uncanny as the castration complex, with its unreasonable anxiety, could have originated only in the dim, irrational past and come down to us mainly in inherited memory traces; that in its present form it could not possibly have appeared in man at a late and high stage of development and been absent in more primitive times.

Our vision may be further blunted by thinking of initiatory circumcision as if it were the same as circumcision in our own culture. But in Western society it is imposed on a helpless infant, to whom it offers no clear advantages and to whom it is thus undesirable and threatening (I ignore medical reasons or rationalizations).

True, circumcision in the first days of life is unlikely to make much difference, psychologically. But in our society many boys learn about circumcision at some point in their nursery school years. This is the period in which they are grappling with Oedipal problems and with the difference between the sexes. By this time the parents are also established for most of them as potentially threatening figures, because it is an age, more than any other age, when the child is forced to obey and feels terribly threatened because he cannot care for himself when he does disobey. Thus he is apt to learn about his circumcision at a time when his parents appear more demanding and more threatening to him than at almost any other period of his life.

It is also possible that Freud and his early followers came to the conclusions they did because the circumcised patients whom they analyzed were predominantly, if not entirely, Jewish; that is, they were circumcised in infancy. The now widespread practice of circumcising all boy babies for medical reasons was not yet common procedure. For these Jewish patients circumcision was therefore more complex. It was part of being subject to religious discrimination, and part of a belief in an Old Testament deity who described himself as jealous and vengeful. In short, this particular group of boys learned of being circumcised (when the rest of the population was not) at about the same time that they became aware of their Jewishness, and when their Oedipal difficulties with their fathers were at a peak. Taken together, it is not surprising that circumcision was most suitably connected with a feeling that those who inflicted it had it in for the boy.* Among the tribes that practice circumcision it takes place at a much older age, when the youngster is often quite able to care for himself, when he knows much more about life, about his parents and their intentions. Hence it should appear far less threatening and the men who impose it less formidable. Among some tribes it is also clearly recognized that unless the boy understands the positive purposes of circumcision he is too young for the ceremony. One is tempted to add: because it might lead to castration anxiety rather than sexual freedom.

Bohannan reports that "One woman, whose very young grandson was being circumcised, kept her back to the operation and wondered to me nervously whether he wasn't perhaps a little too young: he couldn't possibly understand as yet that the real reason it was being done was to enable him to become a man, marry, and have children: perhaps they should have waited until the child was a bit older."[32] For such youngsters circumcision may simply be likened to the many scarifications that accompany pubertal initiation rites, all of which bring higher status and other advantages, including the conviction that they make the initiate more attractive to the opposite sex.

Even in our own society it is possible to find examples of painful scarifications, inflicted by parental figures, that do not add to castration anxiety or have sex-inhibiting consequences. Consider the girl who undergoes plastic surgery to improve her appearance. Such an operation may be potentially as painful as circumcision, but the girl may make little of the physical pain in view of the pleasure she hopes will result. Plastic surgery may indeed be a traumatic experience and, in our society, an experience likely to activate much castration anxiety. But does that mean it must lead to less sexual freedom and greater submission to the parent? The psychological meaning of the operation seems to derive, instead, from the result expected and from what actually happens.

I knew two young girls who underwent rhinoplasty. Their cases were very similar, and one of them may serve as an example. Among this girl's deeper and largely unconscious motives were guilt, masochism, and doubts about her femininity. But the conscious reason for surgery was her desire for sexual success, as it appears to be the con-

* See the Appendix for further discussion of infant circumcision.

scious reason for circumcision in preliterate society. The final results of the operation support the idea that the conscious reasons won out, although that may have been because the operation also satisfied unconscious needs.

Before rhinoplasty the girl had seen herself as an ugly duckling (not without some reason, although except for her nose she was not much below the average in attractiveness and had many good friends of both sexes), and, at the age of about twenty, was still very dependent on her parents. Immediately after the operation and before her marriage, she broke away from her parents and achieved a degree of independence she had never thought possible. She had not expected this to result from the surgery and was astonished that it did. The belief that she had become a desirable sex object—and possibly also the satisfaction of unconscious masochistic desires and a need for punishment, of which she remained unaware—seemed to bring psychological independence from the parents even before full sex enjoyment. Thus a traumatic physical experience brought psychological independence, if not maturity.

It might be said that this girl had deep feelings of inferiority which she had rationalized by blaming it all on her big nose. She believed that removal of this external source of inferiority feelings would and did bring emotional well-being. Though much more complex psychological mechanisms were undoubtedly at work, her final experience more than compensated for the surgical trauma.

Soon after her operation, she was married, made good sexual and marital adjustments, and since then has lived a rather happy life. Moreover, with heightened self-esteem and greater satisfaction of her narcissism, she became less masochistic and guilty. Her supposed ugliness had made her afraid of other associations and had forced her into unsatisfactory, ambivalent, and guilty dependence on her mother. After surgery she was able to strike out for herself. This made her less dependent on, hence less disappointed by her mother, and less hostile and guilty. All this, and most of all her sexual success, she experienced as the result of surgery, which she felt had finally changed her into a woman.

It may be suggested that this proves that plastic surgery is experienced as castration; that through it the girl got rid of (or was deprived of) an imagined penis and so was forced into femininity. If the operation permitted her to resolve her ambivalence about femininity—and thus helped her to accept and to succeed in the feminine role —the parallel to initiation, which I believe helps the initiate to accept the mature sex role, would be striking.

Whatever else it may show, this example indicates that physical traumata which in our society would more commonly be experienced as a castration threat can within another psychological constellation acquire a very different meaning and have other consequences than to increase sexual anxiety.

Durkheim has pointed out how ritual cruelties are commonly executed on a particular organ or tissue in the belief that this will stimulate its vitality. For example, among some Australians the novices are bitten severely in the scalp to make the hair grow; others make small wounds in their arms with heated sticks in order to become skillful in making fire or to acquire the strength to carry heavy loads of wood; by amputating part of the index finger of one hand, Warramunga girls think they make the hand more successful at finding yams.[33] This belief may also help explain the initiates' desire for, as well as fear of, the impending mutilation. It suggests how positively they may view the operation and its later consequences.

Such operations as those noted by Durkheim probably invest the particular organ with a large amount of libido. That this is ordinarily the case in surgical operations is a well-known fact, and Nunberg has stressed it in regard to circumcision.[34] Still one might ask in the case of the young American girl: how can investing the nose with libido lead to better heterosexual adjustments? A possible explanation is that before the operation this girl had withdrawn libido from an external world that disappointed her. Feeling ugly, she may have turned back toward herself a great deal of emotional energy in order to maintain self-acceptance and inner integration.

After surgery libido may at first have been drawn toward the nose. But while in the hospital the girl had a new experience: what she had invested with libido was so invested by others too. The organ which had up to then stood in the way of gratification from others suddenly became a source of gratification. The surgeon, the nurses, her friends showed great interest in and concern with it. The nose suddenly received attention and praise. Later this investment of libido in one part of her body came to be distributed over the rest—perhaps under the influence of the flattering attention that was now paid to at least one part of her body. She now felt more attractive and hence was more attractive. This new feeling may at first have been the consequence of narcissistic libido, but the final effect of the interest and approval of other persons was to free libido for investment in object relations.

This example throws further light on the difference between infant circumcision, as practiced in civilized society, and initiatory circumcision in preliterate society. In infancy, assuming that at such an early age libido is drawn to the organ by circumcision, there can be no beneficial consequences—it is pain, without subsequent pleasure. In adolescent circumcision, libidinal investment of the penis soon leads to gratification, since greater sex enjoyment is promised and often coitus follows soon after the operation.

Higher social status and its consequent sense of social well-being also follow. In taking *post* for *propter* the newly circumcised boys may assume that the libidinal investment of the genitals, which may first have resulted from pain, brought about the change in social status; and their masculinity (or at least the importance of their penes) is further impressed on them.

Approaching the problem from entirely different viewpoints, other authors also have stressed that ritual mutilations lead to an investment of the organ with great significance. Durkheim feels certain that what he calls "the cruel rites of circumcision and subincision" have the object of conferring particular powers on the genital organ.[35] In calling these ceremonies "cruel," rather than painful, however, he leaves the frame of reference of the people who practice them. Powerful they undoubtedly are, and probably also painful, but nothing the people say or do permits us to conclude that they experience these rituals as cruel. Once more we see the Western observer imposing his own value judgments.

Nobody I know has regarded cosmetic plastic surgery as "cruel"; even the pain seems reduced by the desire with which the operations are approached. The person who complains volubly about everyday suffering may minimize great pain when the emotions connected with it are strongly positive.

If the girl in our example was more than willing to pay

the price of surgical trauma for beauty, if many other modern women eagerly undergo painful plastic surgery for the same reason, how can we doubt that the pre-literate boy is ready to endure as much in order to prove that he is a man among the men of his tribe?

That boys often look forward to initiation and circumcision with pleasurable though somewhat anxious anticipation may be inferred from their behavior. Among the Masai of South East Africa, for a few weeks preceding circumcision the boys decorate themselves lavishly and dance in their own and neighboring villages, expressing their happiness because they will soon enter the privileged class of initiates.[36] Nandi boys and girls similarly anticipate it with pleasure.[37]

The Tikopia, among whom the operation consists of a slitting of the upper surface of the foreskin (superincision), make no attempt "to terrify [the initiates] or to inflict upon them any pain beyond what is unavoidable. The operation is in no sense designed as an ordeal to try their manly fortitude, or to harden them to bear pain. To the Tikopia the modification of the sexual organ is its primary aim, and these other aspects are definitely minimized as far as possible."[38] This statement of the primary aim is typical; the ulterior purpose has to do with sexual intercourse, or, I might extrapolate, human fertility.

Bohannan reports that: "Nowadays, particularly in central Tivland [Nigeria], many young, uncircumcised boys—usually at the age of about eight—take themselves to the dispensaries and ask the dispensers to circumcise them. In such a case, no magical ceremonies are performed before the operation, and the dispenser dresses the wound and applies European medicines until the wound is healed. I know one Kparve youngster of about seven years who asked and received his mother's permission to visit her parents; near their compound was a dispensary, and when he returned home three weeks later, he had been circumcised, and considered it a special 'surprise' for his mother and brothers."[39]

That the boys are fearful of circumcision is what one might expect. In our own society, many a malingerer has shot himself in the foot or mangled a finger to escape military service. He wished for the consequence of his action (freedom from military service), but was very afraid of the mutilating act and showed great pain when inflicting it on himself. If the Tiv boys viewed circumcision as castration, they would probably fight back with all their might.

"Today," adds Bohannan, "Tiv say that it is impossible for a man to have sexual relations before he has been circumcised. If one points out that this was apparently not the case if the myth of Tiv ancestor is to be believed, and that it is certainly not true about several of the surrounding tribes, Tiv say that you are quite right, but that in Tivland no woman will consent to sexual relations with any man who is uncircumcised, therefore their initial statement was correct. Tiv women say that the idea of sexual relations with an uncircumcised man is repugnant, and insist quite adamantly that no woman whatever would sleep with such a man. Some give reasons of cleanliness; most, however, phrase their distaste in terms of fastidiousness. We could find no other reason than this given by Tiv for the fact that they circumcise all normal males. Extensive questioning reveals no trace of religious motivation, though Tiv have, in order to make this point clear, contrasted their own customs with those of Mohammedans, among whom a religious reason is said (by Tiv) to be present. We could find no Tiv who would give a ritual reason of any sort for cimcumcision. Circumcision is, however, associated in a symbolic way with adult male status."

Contrary to our views, which connect circumcision with neurotic castration anxiety, the Tiv consider it a sign of neurosis to be afraid of circumcision. This became apparent to Bohannan when Tiv discussed the few neurotic males who were not circumcised. "Such a man did or had none of the things which are prized attributes of normal adult man: having a compound of one's own, prosperous farms, wives, and children, performing ceremonies for control of fetishes (*akombo*) and seeking prestige. Tiv added, as a sort of summary to such a recital, 'He has none of these things; he is not circumcised.' "[40]

Fertility, the Basic Rite

BEHIND MANY HUMAN RITUALS lies an interest in fertility, both the fertility of human beings and of their sources of food.[1] And indeed, the economic and social well-being of any people depends on the regeneration of its food supply. In preliterate societies that have no means of rational control over their animal, plant, or human fertility, its people tend to rely on magico-religious ceremonial to affect it.

The society we are here most concerned with, that of the Australian aborigines, represents a cultural stage that predates the beginning of animal breeding or agriculture; both of these techniques presuppose a concentrated interest in fertility, with first the desire, and later the ability, to assure procreation. Nevertheless, the Australians are very much concerned with procreation, and much of their ritual centers around it. "The Aborigine has no granaries, but he has, if we may use the term, these 'spiritual' storehouses, in that they insure him against starvation, and give him a sense of security and confidence in regard to his food-supply for the coming year."[2] The story the aborigines tell is as follows: "As the totemic ancestors passed through the country they left stones or sometimes a tree, each of which is supposed to contain the *gunin* of some animal, bird, fish, reptile, tuber, and so on. . . . By rubbing one of these or striking it with brushes and uttering a spell, the *gunin* will go forth and cause the species with which it is associated to multiply."[3]

This is evidence both of the resources and desires of a surviving preliterate people in relation to fertility. We have less exact but suggestive evidence that paleolithic man was likewise concerned with procreation. But the subject of greatest interest here is not merely whether and to what degree religious rites were connected in early times with a desire for abundance of animals and men—and hence with procreation and childbirth—but whether this function was thought to be female or male. In the Old Testament, where a male God promises to make males numerous as the stars, it was clearly a male function. Sometimes it is assumed that the rites of the early hunters were masculine in nature, and that the feminine element came only with agriculture. There is indeed ample evidence that, with the development of agriculture, women came to play a very important role in fecundity ceremonies. It was believed that the livelihood of the tribes depended on women and on the rites they performed; that without these, no crops would grow.

In recent years, ever more abundant evidence comes to light suggesting that even in the days of the earliest hunters man's mind was concerned not only with conjuring up the animals he hunted for food but also with magically increasing their number. It seems, for example, that we shall have to revise our earlier notions of the meaning of paleolithic cave paintings of animals and of so-called hunting scenes. Originally these paintings were thought to represent magic efforts to assure good hunting of the animals depicted. Now it is believed that, possibly in association with rituals, they were efforts to stimulate animal procreation. Raphael, for example, says that among the main purposes of the paintings "besides the magic of hunting there was the magic fertility." He also discusses drawings in which "animals pictured one inside the other may represent pregnancy."[4]

These relatively recent analyses do not settle the question of whether any ceremonies—increase or otherwise—were performed, and if so, whether they were performed by men or by women. Beyond this remains the incontrovertible fact of the paintings' location. Since these hunters lived in caves, it is natural that the paintings should be found on cave walls. But the caves contain rooms that are easily accessible, as well as others that can only be reached with great difficulty; and it was the latter that the artists generally chose. Many authors have commented with surprise on the fact that the paintings are so commonly located in almost inaccessible places. In reading their reports, I was most impressed by the tortuous paths leading to the pictures, by the fact that they are hidden behind serious obstacles and often cannot be reached except by crawling through narrows.

Levy, for example, speaks of "the formidable nature" of the long, narrow, slippery corridors, often crossed by waterfalls, and the chimneys that must be negotiated to reach the halls of the pictures. To illustrate: The chamber of Clotilde can only be approached on hands and knees. At one point the passage to Font-de-Gaune becomes a tunnel through which a large person can pass only with great difficulty. To reach La Pasiega the visitor passes through a manhole below which a river runs, and the painted animals can only be seen above the precipices that border it.[5] Levy and others insist that if the purpose of the paintings had been simply to assure success in hunting (not to speak of "pure" artistic creation), their placement at such inaccessible locations would remain incomprehensible. Many who have explored them have concluded that their location must have had a specific purpose. As Marett said, no one would dream of hedging round a mere picture gallery with such trying turnstiles.[6]

All this suggests to me one possibility: that an effort was made to reproduce the setting in which procreation takes place. If so, then to crawl through narrow, wet channels on entering may have represented how access is gained to the secret place of procreation; on leaving, the process of birth might have been reenacted symbolically. The paintings were therefore executed at places that may have been viewed as representing the womb, where animals come into existence. So it is possible that early man was creating a new animal, the painted one, in a place which to him represented the womb, so that the real animal might be induced to do likewise.

This interpretation of the cave paintings' location has not been suggested, to my knowledge, by those who have written about them, but Levy at least sees a definite and close connection between the pictures, the rituals of early man, and their emphasis on birth, death, and rebirth. She stresses how often gravid female figures can be found among the remnants of the same paleolithic culture in the same places, and notes that many of these figures and other female symbols are found lying face downward. She suggests that some significance may have been attached, even before the beginnings of agriculture, to contact with the earth—that, in fact, the cave had already become "a Mother."[7]

Among modern preliterate people, Levy stresses the importance of the ritual re-enactment of traveling a long, winding path, and how important are the experiences that can only be had in caves. Speaking about the Australian aborigines, and quoting Spencer and Gillen, she says:

"In the well-known ceremony for the propagation of the witchetty-grub, the winding march is taken to the sacred caves in which stones have been deposited to represent this insect and her eggs. After contact has been established, first between the stones and their own persons, later with the sacred rock . . . they return to enter the cave-like 'chrysalis' which has meanwhile been constructed at the camp. . . . From this they emerge singing the re-born grub. . . .

"This applies equally to the initiation ceremonies of the boys and girls, whose period of seclusion seems to have been passed in the bush, with the exception of novice magicians who repaired to a cave for their sleep of death and rebirth."[8]

Levy leaves little doubt that these caves represent the womb in which the initiates are born again.[9] I shall not follow much further her speculations on the connection between a mother goddess and the pregnant female figures, beyond the following quotations:

"It does appear possible, indeed, that on all the continents where later civilizations did not influence her development, the 'Mother Goddess' disappeared from the religious system, as her images disappeared from the Magdalenian hearths. In South Eastern Europe, on the other hand, in the North African hinterland and Western Asia, the great discoveries of the succeeding eras, especially the domestication of animals and the cultivation of corn, imparted to this conception an increasingly deep significance. . . .

"The little statues of mammoth ivory, stone, or conglomerate, represent in general an upright woman with small featureless bent head and feeble arms usually laid upon her huge breasts, with very wide or deep hips, loins and abdomen, and legs dwindling to small or non-existent feet. . . .

"Some cult of human fertility is indicated, which was brought into touch with the rites for animal reproduction in the caves. This cult appears, on the evidence of the statuettes, to have originated among the Aurignacians of Eastern Europe and spread westward, where the figures are found in smaller numbers, occasionally possessing great formal artistry."[10]

The importance of the gravid female figures is further emphasized by the fact that no male figures have been found.[11] This is consistent with Braidwood's findings in the excavation of the village of Jarmo, which he considers the earliest permanent settlement of man; at Jarmo there was a combination of a hunting and agricultural setting, a community in transition toward what Braidwood calls "incipient agriculture and animal domestication." There, too, gravid female figures are among the predominant ritual artifacts, the most characteristic being "a seated pregnant woman with rather fat buttocks—probably a 'mother goddess' symbol of fertility." No male or phallic figures were discovered.[12]

We have no evidence that paleolithic man practiced circumcision, as the modern hunters and food gatherers of Australia do. But evidence from prehistory does indicate that the earliest man had a deep and abiding interest in fertility, and that if he had a ritual life, the ceremony of increase was probably its most essential part. Great effort went into the creation of pregnant female figures of the Venus of Willendorf type.

In Australian aboriginal society a relationship clearly exists between the rites of fertility and initiation. In mythical times, according to Strehlow, they were not separated at all, there being only one great series of ceremonies to initiate the young and to assure totemic increase.[13] In modern times, during the initiation of aboriginal boys, various totemistic ceremonies take place to assure an abundance of food animals. Seemingly more important even than circumcision or subincision is the fact that for the first time boys are permitted to witness the fertility ceremonies. Thus the puberty rites of boys among these people is an initiation into the secret of how to influence magically the increase of food animals and edible fruits.

On these occasions, men decorate themselves (*i.e.,* change themselves symbolically) to represent the animal they wish to procreate abundantly; it seems plausible that the changes they make on their own bodies have the same purpose—to assure their own fertility. The difference is that the change into the animal is only temporary, the decorations being discarded or washed off after the ceremony is over, while the changes made on their penes are permanent. The fact that among certain Australian tribes the initiation ceremony always takes place before harvest[14] may also be significant. Thus the puberty rite is probably meant to assure procreation of the human animal, while other increase rites, from the *intichiuma* of the Australians to the buffalo dances of the Sioux, encourage the multiplication of food animals.

If we are allowed to draw inferences from some modern preliterate societies to paleolithic man, available evidence would justify the conclusion that increase rites were the most important ceremonies of the earliest human societies and that initiation ceremonies may be mainly special subforms.*

During the ceremonies of the Uli cult of New Ireland (neither an initiation ritual nor an initiation society) elaborate male figures called Ulis are carved. They are powerfully proportioned, bearded figures, whose oversized breasts and phalli express the power of fertility, the cult which they serve. They are not viewed as hermaphroditic; on the contrary, they are considered the more male because they also possess female sex powers and characteristics. The ceremonies in which these figures were used sometimes lasted a year, and included dances in which the men tied carved female breasts around their chests. These rites were extremely sacred and all females were excluded from them. Uli figures were never discarded, but were carefully preserved for future ceremonies. Nevermann says that both the Uli figures and the dances seem to have originated in a fertility cult,[15] and Krämer adds that the oversized breasts and phallus express the great power of fecundity.[16] Thus men have used other methods than manipulation of the penis by which to claim a greater share in procreation.

Certain of the Goulbourn Islanders who have had considerable contact with white civilization and have come to understand a little better the male contribution to procreation, have evolved an interesting variation of the

---

* By the time anthropologists came to observe these rites, their order of importance may have become reversed, with initiation rites the more widespread and elaborate, until they could well be regarded as the central rites of primitive society. Here the relative importance of rituals merely followed the development of society. In our own society, for example, fertility seems again to be the most elaborate ritual of our private lives. According to religious precepts and the official moral code, procreation must not occur without marriage. Thus, at least in official doctrine, our principal ritual is concerned with procreation, if not with fertility.

mother goddess. The Berndts, in discussing the fertility goddess and main deity of these tribes (who practice neither circumcision nor subincision), report that the beliefs and ceremonies surrounding her are less vivid than elsewhere, rituals and beliefs connected with the snake having been superimposed.[17] At this moment, the religious beliefs of these tribes may thus be in transition. The predominance of a female fertility goddess may be giving way to the predominance of a male (or bisexual) fertility symbol. The original concept of the fertility goddess, however, is neither lost nor seriously obscured. One of the central rites of this transitional cult is the reenactment of the fight for predominance between the male and the female principle. The female tries to assert her superiority, but the male deity, by means of a phallic symbol, succeeds in taking revenge on her.[18] Still, many details emphasize that the ritual was, and still is, closely related to the mother goddess. For example:

"At Goulbourn Island the sacred ground is the body of the Mother, and the 'outside' (secular) name of the *'u:ba:r* [phallic symbol] is *'kamo:mo,* which is the ordinary word for a mother. It is said that she comes out when she hears it is ceremonial time; her spirit enters the *'u:ba:r,* which is made and erected . . . for the purpose, and she 'talks'—that is, the beating of the *'u:ba:r.* She is calling for everybody to come, but only the men can enter her presence and her body. . . . Should the beating [of the *'u:ba:r*] be stopped, her spirit will go also and the ritual will lose its potency; she maintains the essence of sanctity, and gives the participants power to perform their ritual actions and dancing. It is she who attends to the increase of the natural species."[19]

Even in the snake ritual, therefore, everything depends on the female fertility goddess. While this ritual may illustrate a transition from a maternal to a phallic religion, under the influence of a growing knowledge of procreation, we are here mainly concerned with developments that may have taken place before such masculine gods appeared. Phallicism does not seem to exist in a society such as that of the Australians who believe that the man's contribution to procreation lies only in "finding" the spirit child, and his "making a way" for the child to be born. It should be stressed once more that their ritual life must be understood in terms of their utter dependence on the chance multiplication of their food sources; animals are not abundant, and the people lack the knowledge needed for agriculture or animal husbandry. Thus their concern with fertility is almost inevitable.

Ritual Surgery

Castration

WHETHER OR NOT there is an intrinsic link between castration and circumcision, they are now so closely connected in the thinking of many persons that a discussion of puberty rites must also consider castration. As an institution, castration appeared comparatively late in history, among relatively sophisticated peoples. It was then performed by the castrate to please, or to make himself more like, an overpowering mother figure.

Historical reviews tell us little about whether, or how commonly, castration actually took place in preliterate society. Browe[1] and others believe that the custom probably originated with the Hittites and spread first to the Semitic and then to other Asian and European civilizations. Like other authors, including Weigert-Vowinkel, Browe stresses the practice of castration among the priests of the mother goddesses as part of their rites. Compared with this ritual castration in the service of a female deity, castration as a punishment inflicted by men on men for religious reasons, or by law, is a comparatively late institution. In the Middle Ages it was part of the talion law, with no special sexual connotations. Among the Germans at this period it was a punishment for sacreligious acts, but only as part of total dismemberment.[2]

In combat or war, however, castration appears in much earlier times as the toll exacted by the victor from his defeated enemy. In Egypt this form of it was known in both religious and military practice; witness the eternal fight between Horus and Set in which Horus castrated Set for tearing out Horus' eye.[3] Similar tales of castrating the vanquished occur in other mythologies, particularly the Greek. The victor's main purpose was to gain for himself the masculine power of his victim.

In Egypt, killing and castrating the conquered in war was later supplemented by the custom of creating eunuchs who could act as servants, especially in the harem. Similarly, the Persians under Darius castrated the handsomest boys after the conquests of Chios, Lesbos, and Tenedos, and then used them as eunuchs or for homosexual pleasure.[4] In the Western Hemisphere, castration was known at least to the Carib-speaking natives of the Antilles. According to Roth, they "practised in on their boy prisoners, who were subsequently fattened for the table."[5] Castration in later times, for artistic purposes (to retain high adult voices in the papal choir) is of little interest here.

Thus the known history of the castration of men by men, though meager, shows no connection with age-grading ceremonies at puberty and no direct connection with jealousy between father and son or with any psychological motives connected with the Oedipal situation or the incest taboo. Speculation based on these connections remain unsupported by factual evidence.

The story of castration in the service of the great maternal deities is different. There we are in no doubt that the mother goddesses required emasculation as the price of grace. Weigert-Vowinkel has summarized for us Daly's analysis of Hindu mythology as it pertains to the castration complex. In it she refers to the "flood of uncontrollable fear" of the castrating maternal divinity which permeates that literature. She suggests that conflicts characterized by the castration theme, which were also prominent in the myths of the Trobrianders, may be typical of matriarchal societies, the myths having been invented after the rites, to explain them.[6]

Of the rites of the maternal deities, those of Cybele are perhaps the best known. They tell us that ". . . at the peak of exaltation on *deis sanguinis,* March 24, every one of the Galloi [priests of Cybele] voluntarily castrated himself by cutting off the entire genitals with a consecrated stone knife. . . . The use of bronze or iron was forbidden for this act. Women who dedicated themselves to the goddess in like manner cut off one or both breasts."[7] Even in ancient times it was assumed that the command to use only stone implements for self-mutilation testified to the great antiquity of the practice.

Here too, self-mutilation was not restricted to one sex, just as male circumcision is often paralleled by the manipulation and mutilation of female organs. The Cybele rites reflect deviate tendencies in both men and women; either an inordinate desire to be, or an extreme fear of, the opposite sex. Still, mutilation of the men was much more severe than that of women; the male sacrificed his primary sex characteristics, the female only the secondary ones.

During the course of the rites ". . . the flood of orgiastic emotion even spread to the onlookers and they, too, castrated themselves. With their genitals in their hands, the worshippers ran through the streets and threw them into some house, from which they then received women's clothing, according to custom."[8] Considering what the castrates received for the gift of their genitals, it seems legitimate to infer that they threw them to or at women, who, in return, gave them female garments.*

Once the devotees of the mother goddess were castrated, their genitals and masculine clothing were carried into the bridal chamber of Cybele. Thereafter, they wore only women's clothing, were anointed and wore their hair long. Latin and Greek writers usually speak of them in the feminine gender.[9]

This example of ritual castration, and many others not mentioned here, indicates that it was exacted by maternal figures as a sign of devotion and submission on the part of their male followers and particularly of the priests who were closest in their service. Of women, other signs of devotion were required; only the priests had to approximate the other sex in attire and behavior. Their becoming "female" after self-mutilation had no counterpart in what was expected of women serving the goddess.†

* Fantasies about similar acts occur today. The wish that a man should cut off his genitals and throw them to a woman was expressed by a schizoid pubertal girl living at the Orthogenic School. She had only recently begun to menstruate when one day, in a public park near the School, she observed a man in the bushes who was urinating, or exposing himself to her, or both. Turning to her woman counselor and another girl she said with great glee, "He'll cut off his penis and throw it at us." Fantasies about boys who are turned into girls and then have to wear female clothing are so common among neurotic children, both boys and girls, that they need hardly be mentioned. While such ideas reflect castration anxiety, they originate in even earlier experiences, as discussed in Chapter 3.

† In this context, but without wishing to speculate too far, I should like to point out that it was approximately in the geographical area where the mother goddesses were worshipped that the use of harem eunuchs was widespread. The explanation generally given is that eunuchs are safe as harem servants because they cannot have sexual relations with the women in their care. But if this were the only reason, one might ask why female servants were not used. Although it is perhaps far-fetched, the possibility might be considered that this custom was a remnant of the rites of the mother goddess. It might also be based partly on the women's desire to have subservient to them men who had first been deprived of their male sexuality. The castrated priests of Cybele were, after all, as much servants of the mother goddess as eunuchs were the servants of women in the harem.

The fact that the mutilation was self-chosen and self-inflicted suggests that the psychological motivation came from deeper layers of the personality than would be true if it were imposed by others. It also indicates that men were ready and willing to become "female" in order to share women's superior powers.

Circumcision

While history does not furnish a connection between actual castration and the castration complex, that does not prove there is no link between castration and circumcision. Parallel to the history of castration in the worship of the Magna Mater are the biblical story of Zipporah and the numerous myths current in modern preliterate societies. According to these, it was women again who imposed circumcision on men, a belief that is also suggested by some forms of postcircumcision behavior. For example, revenge by men against women for intended or actual circumcision is acted out among the Kikuyu of western Africa: the newly circumcised boys, in groups of fifteen or twenty, attack and rape old women and finally kill them.[10]

Many features of initiation rites suggest that they are in part sacrificial offerings to mother figures. Spencer and Gillen (and others) have reported numerous instances in which the initiates present their foreskins, blood, or teeth to women. Among the Western Arunta, the foreskin is presented to a sister of the novice, who dries it, smears it with red ochre, and wears it suspended from her neck.[11] In some tribes, after a boy has been circumcised, the blood from the wound is collected in a shield and taken to his mother, who drinks some of it, and gives food to the man who brought it to her.[12] Among the Australian Binbinga tribe, the blood running from the subincision wound was collected by the subincised boy on a piece of bark and taken to his mother.[13] Westermarck reports that the foreskin of the circumcised Ait Yusi boy is taken to his mother who fastens it to the little stick that supports her spindle, puts it on her head, and dances with it. Among some related peoples, the boy's mother swallows the foreskin.[14]

Swallowing, or oral incorporation, is the most archaic

method of acquiring the desired qualities of an object, if not the object itself. The first positive instinctual behavior toward an attractive object is to lessen the distance between self and object and finally, in the most archaic form, to swallow it; the first negative instinctual behavior toward a repulsive object is to widen the distance and spit it out.[15]

Oral incorporation of parts of the genitals of the other sex also occurs in Liberian Poro initiation. The foreskins are dried and turned over to the woman who has charge of the girls' initiation society, and they are cooked and eaten by all the girls. Similarly, the clitoridi and labia minora removed during the girls' initiation are given to the property man of the Poro society and are cooked and eaten by the boys at circumcision.[16] As is often true of oral incorporation, it is hard to decide which is stronger: the hostile desire to take away from the other sex, or the envious desire to have the incorporated parts. Still a very similar underlying ambivalence seems to exist in societies even so far apart in geography and culture as the Liberian and Australian. In any case the custom leaves little doubt that initiation is greatly concerned with the organs, if not the functions of the other sex.

Among the Tikopia incision of the foreskin takes the place of circumcision. It is performed over a sheet of bark cloth, which is then hung around the neck of an "unmarried mother" (in kinship terms) of the boy. As soon as the wound is bandaged, the boy "is made to stand, the waistcloth he is wearing is removed once again, and he dons a new one. In this he is assisted by the mother's sisters and by the wives of his mother's brothers who have brought the fresh garments. . . . This ceaseless changing of garments has the object of allowing his female relatives to . . . wear around their necks the garments they remove."[17]

Among certain natives of Victoria (Australia), "On arriving at manhood a youth was conducted by three leaders of the tribe into the recesses of the woods. . . . Being furnished with a suitable piece of wood, he knocks out two of the front teeth of his upper jaw, and on returning to the camp gives them to his mother."[18] Collins in his description of this rite does not say definitely who received the teeth, but infers it was women.[19] Spencer and Gillen remark that while many tribes treat the knocking out of teeth as a major ritual, the Central Australian tribes have reduced it to a rudiment that has lost its original significance as applied to men only, and has been extended to women as well.* In the rudimentary Arunta rite, the tooth is thrown in the direction of the camp of the mythical mothers; the authors interpret this to indicate that possibly in early times the mother was entitled to the tooth.[20]

Loeb is convinced that circumcision was originally performed as a sacrifice to a female goddess. He finds it highly improbable that it could have arisen spontaneously from different causes in different parts of the world, since the custom is not of an obvious nature. The wide variety of explanations offered, he feels, should not detract from this fact; with so ancient a practice it was bound to be differently interpreted and rationalized in various places.[21] He follows Barton,[22] who holds that originally all Semitic circumcision was a sacrifice to the goddess of fertility; this placed the child under her protection and consecrated its reproductive powers to her service.[23]

The role of women in receiving the products of mutilation—blood, foreskin, teeth—and the resemblance of such gifts to offerings, is indeed striking. I have spoken of possible reasons why women covet these gifts. But what of the donors? Sacrificial offerings are made for various reasons, whether to placate the gods or in response to demands. But a primary reason is the worshipper's hope of a return for his offering; often a reward much greater than the value of his gift. Thus Australian aboriginal men may present their foreskins to their mothers or sisters partly to ensure the women's good will, or partly to satisfy their demand for circumcision. But we may also infer that the men expect something in return for the sacrifice. As to what that may be we can only speculate. I suggest that

* In view of the opinion (see page 105) that the practice of circumcision may have spread from men to women, a conjecture in support of which little tangible evidence can be presented, it seems worth stressing Spencer and Gillen's conclusion that a custom or ritual connected with initiation loses much of its original meaning when extended to the other sex. Apparently these authors, too, felt that rites of initiation are so closely related to the differences in sex functions between men and women that they must have lost most of their significance when they could be applied to either sex.

it might be a share in women's great and secret power of procreation, a gift that only women can bestow because only women possess it.

Myths on the Origin of Circumcision

Although mythical accounts say that male circumcision was first performed by women, it should be realized that the emotional impact of myths is different in preliterate society than in our own. The events they tell of take place in a past that seems dim and remote, but at the same time eternal, since it also shapes what is done in the present. In their emotional effects, events described in myths have an immediacy in the people's present lives that compare with a young child's experience. To him, figures from fairy tales (witches, ferocious or protecting animals) are often more real or powerful an influence on his emotional life than persons in the real world.

If the myths state that women originally circumcised men, then, in a way, they still do, although the execution may now be vested in men. We may conjecture that if people believe firmly that in mythical times women circumcised boys, and if the operation is now performed by men, they may now experience it as circumcision by *both* women and men. Not only the circumcised boy but the circumcisor too may feel he is taking part in a function that was originally female.

In Murngin tradition, the Wawilak saga is the most important one centering around *rites de passage*. The mythical Wawilak sisters represent the two female sex functions that seem to fascinate men, or both men and women, most—one sister is menstruating, the other pregnant. The myth states simply and directly: "Circumcision started when those two women tried to cut their boys" in mythical times.[24] It was only when the male ancestors dreamed of them that the rites passed into the hands of men.[25]

According to other myths women introduced or changed the tool with which circumcision is performed. In one region of Australia the mythical account states that women introduced the stone knife, where a fire stick was used before. These women threw a sharp piece of flint to the men who then began to use it in circumcising boys.[26] Still another myth relates that a woman gave the stone knife to the ancestors for circumcision, and that initiation of men was originally derived from that of women.

In a myth current among the Adnjamatana tribe of South Australia, the originator of circumcision is described as neither male nor female nor human but a semihuman bird, *Jurijurilja,* one of the totemic ancestors. This bird once threw a boomerang, and as it returned, it circumcised the bird and entered the vulvas of his wives, cutting them internally so that they bled. This caused their monthly menstrual periods.[27] Here menstruation is viewed as a consequence of circumcision. The story not only establishes a direct and close connection between circumcision and menstruation; indirectly it suggests that just as procreation in women cannot take place before they begin to menstruate, circumcision is an analogous precondition.

The legend of the Unthippa women, one of the most important myths of the Arunta, tells us that "When [these women] . . . found . . . people . . . about to perform the rite of circumcision upon some . . . boys . . . [the women] took the boys on their shoulders and carried them along with them, leaving them at various spots en route, after performing circumcision on them."[28]* Then the women wandered on until they reached a place where, because of exhaustion from dancing, their sexual organs dropped out, forming deposits of red ochre. Similar stories are told of other mythical women, and "the deposits of red ochre which are found in various parts [of the country] are associated with women's blood . . . Tradition says that . . . women . . . caused blood to flow from the vulva in large quantities, and so formed the deposit of red ochre."[29]

The myth not only asserts that the Unthippa women invented circumcision (a belief acted out in present-day circumcision rites) but also indicates that they bled from or lost their sex organs *after* they had circumcised the boys. If this sequence of events has any meaning, it suggests that bleeding from, or the loss or mutilation of the femal sex organ as in the introcision of girls, is a consequence of (punishment for?) the circumcision of boys.

Red ochre is thus of great importance in puberty rites.

* It should be noted, in reference to remarks on circumcision as a precondition of marriage, that these circumcising women belonged to a group into which, according to the kinship system, any of the boys could have married.

In the thinking of these people, it is not simply symbolic but is actually the mythical women's sex organs or genital blood; thus in its wide ceremonial use red ochre must be viewed as menstrual blood or else very closely related to it.*

The occasion of circumcision is the only one at which women of these tribes are permitted to decorate themselves as warriors and to carry men's weapons. After the novice has sat down among the men, "The women, who had been awaiting his arrival, at once began to dance, carrying shields in their hands. The reason assigned for this is that the mythical Unthippa women . . . also carried shields and . . . the initiation ceremony must commence with an imitation of their dance. . . . (Roth describes the women as decorated after the manner of warriors about to engage in a fight during the early part of the proceedings.) Except in connection with this ceremony women may never carry shields, which are exclusively the property of the men."[30]

" . . . At a later time . . . in the ceremony . . . just before the performance of the actual ceremony [of circumcision] one of the women . . . placing her head between [the novice's] legs suddenly lifts him up on her shoulders and runs off with him, as . . . the *Unthippa* women did, but unlike what happened in the past, the boy is again seized by the men and brought back."[31]

After describing this ceremony, Spencer and Gillen remark that whatever these Unthippa women may have been, the myth indicates that women once played an even more important part in such ceremonies than they do in modern times.[32]

The people of the New Hebrides state explicitly that women invented circumcision. They say that one day a man went into the jungle with his sister. She climbed a breadfruit tree to cut down the ripe fruit with a bamboo. When she had finished she threw down the bamboo, which accidentally cut the man's foreskin. After the man recovered, he had intercourse with a woman, who found it so good that she told another woman; soon this man was in great demand, to the fury of other men; "but their

* Red ochre and other red paints are also used almost universally for decoration or other ritual purposes with no relation to menstrual blood. Red paint may be said to symbolize feminine genital blood only if it is explicitly so stated, as in this case.

women sneer at them and say they need to be like that one. So they pay him to tell the secret. He tells, and they have in such wise cut their children ever after."[33]*

I have already alluded to women's insistence on circumcision, in some preliterate societies, as a prerequisite to coitus, or at least to a permanent sexual relationship. Here I might add that Seligman and Seligman,[34] Larken,[35] and Czekanowski[36] have all commented on how rapidly circumcision is spreading among the African Azande because the women prefer it: "Circumcision is a recent introduction; it is, however, tending to become general in the Congo and is spreading in the Sudan . . . it has no religious significance, but is insisted upon by the women, who like it."[37] A thirteen year old African Sebeyi boy told Bryk that everybody wants to be circumcised because it is beautiful and because the women reject uncircumcised men as sex partners.[38] While prepubertal girls are available to these boys, mature women insist that the men they cohabit with must be circumcised.

Bryk reports a related custom of certain African women. At the very end of the circumcision ceremonies, "His girl comes . . . they talk all through the night. Early in the morning she gives him her hand and in parting says: 'I'll return tonight and then I'll give you my vagina. My dear man. Now I love you truly; . . . you'll come for me, and buy me,' "[39] which is as much as to say, "Marry me." As noted of the Tiv, no sacrificial element is apparent in women's insistence on circumcision before coitus, although it may be present.

Despite the evidence supplied by myths that certain initiation rituals originated not with men but with women, the possibility is not ruled out that they were actually invented by boys or men and inflicted by men. An act that tradition ascribes to women was not necessarily so invented. In animistic thinking, that which caused a person to take a certain action may appear as that which inflicted the action upon him. If women's power to bear young aroused envy in men, then the men may have devised rites for dealing with their envy, and later come to regard women as responsible for originating those rites. And psychologically speaking, they were. Thus the suggestion

* For other myths relating to women's role in originating puberty rites see the discussion of the Kunapipi ritual in the Appendix.

that women originally inflicted circumcision on men should be construed as having either of two meanings: (a) women developed the idea that men should bleed from their genitals (as the girl at the Orthogenic School did) or (b) men envied women's procreative powers and were "forced" to take steps to deal with their envy; these measures they then experienced as imposed by women.

We cannot, in any case, rely on myths, and often not even on the statements made to anthropologists, for any valid explanation of women's role. Resting the blame for the ritual on women might, after all, be an effort to shift responsibility from its rightful place with men. The ritual itself is still our more reliable source. Let us turn, therefore, to subincision, to see if this extreme rite may indicate whether it was originally imposed by men or women; whether any feature of the rite shows the extent to which it is externally imposed and the extent to which it meets the inner needs of youth; whether it seems to be a sacrificial offering to women or mainly the result of a desire to identify with women; and whether it originates in man's envy of women.

Ritual Subincision

Anatomically it is subincision, not circumcision, that is most far-reaching of all initiation ceremonies in making men physically like women. Since it is practiced in only a few areas of the world it is relatively little discussed in the literature, although it involves very radical surgery and probably alters the sensations during coitus. It is described as follows:

"The operation consists essentially in slitting open the whole or part of the penile urethra along the ventral or under surface of the penis. The initial cut is generally about an inch long, but this may subsequently be enlarged so that the incision extends from the glans to the root of the scrotum, in this way the whole of the under part of the penile urethra is laid open. The latter form of the operation is universal among the Central tribes [of Australia]. As one proceeds outwards the intensity of the operation becomes reduced, until we meet with forms which strongly resemble the condition of hypospadias, that is, forms in which a small slit is made in the urethra towards either the glans or the scrotum, or both."[40]

Subincision also interferes with the ability to direct the stream of urine, and afterwards men urinate in the squatting position as women do. True, the urination posture depends to some degree on custom: among the Pilagá, men stand to urinate in the forest but squat to urinate in the village compound, while the women always use the standing posture;* and in some African and Filipino tribes that do not subincise, the squatting position is the only or preferred one for men. Still, the behavior of most human beings and of some animals suggest that the urinating position is based mainly on physiology. In most societies, in any case, next to childbirth and menstruation, the difference in function between the sexes is demonstrated most obviously by the difference in urination posture. Certainly it seems to be noted by children, and to interest them, almost as early as the difference in the sex organs.

Subincision among the Arunta may take place five or six weeks after circumcision, depending on the time needed for recovery from the initial operation. In other tribes, the elapsed time may be much longer. From this ceremony women are excluded, and it proceeds, in part, as follows:

" . . . As soon as ever [the novice] was in position another man sat astride of his body, grasped the penis and put the urethra on the stretch. The operator then approached and quickly, with a stone knife, laid open the urethra from below . . . When all was over the [newly initiated] were led to one side while they squatted over shields into which the blood was allowed to drain . . . and from which it is emptied into the centre of a fire which is made for the purpose. . . . As a result of the operation . . . micturition is always . . . performed in a squatting position. . . .

"It very often happens that, as soon as the operation has been performed on a novice, one or more of the younger men present, who have been operated on before, stand up and voluntarily undergo a second operation," considering that the incision has not been carried far enough. "Standing out on the clear space . . . with legs wide apart and hands behind his back, the man shouts out . . . '*Mura* [wife's mother] mine, come and cut my

* Personal communication of Jules Henry.

subincision down to the root.'. . . . Most men . . . undergo
the second operation and some come forward a third time,
though a man is often as old as thirty or forty-five before
he submits to this second operation."[41]

There are no accounts from these tribes of men request-
ing circumcision or circumcising themselves. Thus, while
the minor operation of circumcision is nearly always performed by others, the more radical subincision, like ritual
castration in the service of the great maternal deities, is
occasionally self-inflicted or, more often, inflicted on the
subject at his request. We might therefore infer that subincision too, is more self-motivated than circumcision.

While the Arunta say that circumcision originated with
the Unthippa women, no direct connection between subincision and mythical females is reported. Nevertheless,
a connection is suggested by the subincised men's behavior on the morning following the operation:

"At daylight on the morning of the next day the men
provide themselves with fire-sticks and, surrounding the
young man, conduct him to the women. . . . When the
party is within a short distance of the women . . . the
young man steps out from the centre of the group and
throws his boomerang high up in the direction of the spot
at which his mother was supposed to have lived in mythical times. This throwing of the boomerang in the direction of the mythical mother's camp . . . occurs [also] during the performance of . . . ceremonies . . . which accompany the knocking out of teeth."[42]

Such attack against the mythical mother may represent
either a desire for revenge or an effort on the young man's
part to protect himself against a danger. It might also be
construed as symbolically putting women in their place,
once the ritual mutilation has occurred. Whatever the
reason, the fact remains that immediately after subinci-
sion(or the knocking out of teeth which in some tribes re-
places circumcision or subincision), a symbolic attack is
carried out against the symbolic mother. This time the
men do not use relatively innocuous pieces of bark, as
they do when the women try to overrun the circumcision
ground earlier in the ceremonies. Now the most potent
weapon of the tribe is used. And while all the men together threw bark at the women, this time only the victim
throws the boomerang; it seems to be less a purely cere-

monial act and more seriously meant as a symbol of personal revenge or attack.

Spencer and Gillen were puzzled by the custom, though they tried to rationalize it within the then prevalent frame of reference—i.e., that the purpose of initiation was to enter manhood and to break the ties between mother and child. Nevertheless, they were dissatisfied with their own explanations and ended by stating that the significance of throwing the boomerang at the mythical mother was difficult to see.

Such behavior would indeed be incomprehensible if aggression were directed against the real mother. It was not she, but the ancient mother who, either directly or through men's envy of women, caused subincision. Whether this suggests that maternal figures inflicted or demanded the operation as a precondition of marriage in prehistoric times; or whether the ancient mother image is that which every man carries within himself from childhood: or whether this figure is the man's childish image of the mother projected into ancient times—these possibilities are irrelevant here. It may still be inferred that subincision is felt to be "caused" by an archaic mother.

Though there are myths of the origin of circumcision, there are none, to my knowledge, explaining subincision, and the Arunta natives have no notion of its beginnings; Spencer and Gillen say that it is equivalent to the opening of the vulva.[43] Otherwise they feel it is useles to speculate.[44] Instead they quote Roth, who remarked on the subincision of men "that, on the principle of a form of mimicry, the analogous sign was inflicted on the male to denote corresponding fitness on his part."[45] This statement of Roth's struck me as one of the deepest insights into the whole problem.

Among these tribes, the fertility of flora and fauna is the very essence of life and livelihood, and initiation is itself an increase ritual. Yet these people understand very little of the physiology of human procreation or the male role in it. Opening the vagina is supposed to facilitate conception, and perhaps it seemed plausible that the wider the opening, the more likely conception and the easier childbirth. It is much harder to understand how operations on the penis were expected to influence procreation.

How little the Australians know about the actual

process of procreation may be illustrated by the following report:

"I investigated the problem as exhaustively as possible, and these natives in spite of over thirty years contact with the white had still no idea of the true relation between sexual intercourse and conception. The aborigines asserted that a young girl could not bear children; after puberty conception only occurred when a man, generally her husband, found a spirit child. Questioned on the function of sexual intercourse natives admitted that it prepared the way for the entry of the spirit child. 'Him made 'em road . . . ; young girl no got 'em road.' Most women believed that the semen remained in the vagina and had nothing to do with the child. 'Him nothing,' was the trenchant reply, when after circuitous inquiry I finally suggested the facts of the case. Several women thought that the semen entered the uterus, and that the embryo floated in it 'like a waterlily,' as one expressed it. Natives with a hint of ridicule for the illogicality of the white would declare impatiently—'All day me bin sleep alonga him. Me no more bin catch 'em picaninny.' A Forest River woman whose child was born some months after her husband's death, advanced this as evidence of the irrelevance of sexual intercourse, which all natives, apart from its preparatory function, regarded simply as an erotic pastime."[46]

Even if the Australians do feel vaguely that the man has something to do with conception, they can never be certain as long as they do not understand the exact processes. When rational knowledge is lacking, dogmatic certainty often fills the gap. But however strongly stated, it never quite eliminates the discomfort of doubt (in institutionalized religion often considered sinful). Doubts are as likely as total absence of knowledge to create insecurity and lead to compensating measures.

Nevertheless, while the people do not understand human procreation, one connection they can establish with certainty: children cannot be born to a woman unless she has first begun to menstruate. "Fitness" on the part of the female is indicated by menstruation. Fitness on the part of the male, however, is by no means so obvious, and what preliterate peoples do not possess in reality, they often try to acquire by magic.

Still referring to Roth, Spencer and Gillen go on to say

that his theory "still leaves unexplained the mutilation of women, and it would seem to be almost simpler to imagine that this was a consequence of the mutilation of the men."[47] It might not only be simpler, but correct. If we assume that the men felt compelled to make themselves similar to women, and if they even dimly realized that they inflicted injuries on themselves to become as fertile as women, then we can understand why, when they failed, they were also angry at women, threw boomerangs at them, and perhaps, after gaining political ascendancy, sought to retaliate by inflicting on women the mutilation men undergo because of them.

Even if men were once forced to submit to subincision, they would hardly continue it and voluntarily request or inflict on themselves a reopening of the wound unless motivated by some inner force. No tribal lore is taught by it. It is no *rite de passage,* since it does not change the person's status. It is a voluntarily chosen mutilation, not a mutilation of the son by the father.

If, however, one begins with the fact that the sub-incision wound is called "vulva," then the operation it-self and the repeated opening of and bleeding from the wound become understandable. Then it appears that the purpose of the ritual may be to reproduce symbolically the female sex organ, while the reopening of the wound may symbolize the periodic phenomenon of menstruation. Statements made by the people themselves confirm such an interpretation. The Murngin say: "The blood that runs from an incision and with which the dancers paint themselves and their emblems is something more than a man's blood—it is the menses of the old Wawilak women . . . 'That blood we put all over those men is all the same as the blood that came from the old woman's vagina. It isn't the blood of those men any more because it has been sung over and made strong. The hole in the man's arm isn't that hole any more. It is all the same as the vagina of that old woman that had the blood coming out of it.' "[48]

Lommel also notes that a red pandanus blossom is inserted into a bleeding subincision wound, the purpose being to keep the slit as red as possible after it has healed.[49] And Roth states that in the Pitta-Pitta and Boulia District dialects the word for an introcised penis means "the one with a vulva."[50] Hogbin reports that the

Wogeo men of New Guinea say that women are automatically cleansed by menstruation, but that men, to guard against illness, periodically incise the penis and allow some blood to flow; an operation which is often called "man's menstruation."[51] Not only the Wogeo but also the Murngin and Dwoma of New Guinea use parallel names for menstrual bleeding and bleeding from the subincision opening.

The negative phase of the menstruation taboo is commonly revealed in the conviction that menstruating women are unclean. In their mimicry, men repeat this negativism in initiation, and among many peoples the novices are considered to be, or make themselves, dirty. Qatu initiates (northern New Hebrides) were secluded for a month; they remained unwashed and came out black with dirt and soot.[52] Among the aborigines of Victoria, the youth's body was daubed with mud and filth, and he had to go through camp for several days and nights throwing filth at everyone he met.[53] Thus boys being initiated contaminate everyone they touch, just as menstruating women are believed to do. In New Guinea, all avoidances imposed on women during the menstrual period also apply to men while they bleed from the subincision wound.[54]

Other observers report similar attitudes. According to Roheim: "The ritual of subincision . . . consists in the older men (the initiators) running backwards and showing their subincision hole. The blood spurts forth from the subincision hole and the youngsters see the great mystery of initiation. It is quite clear what is meant when they call the subincision hole a 'vagina' or a 'penis womb'. . . . They are offering an artificial vagina as compensation for the real one . . ."[55] and "The blood squirting from the penis is called woman, or milk."[56] In another Central Australian tribe, the Urrabuna, subincision is known as *verrupu,* and the vagina is sometimes designated by that term although its proper name is *pintha.*[57]

These and similar data suggested to Bryk that "through subincision the young man is supposed to be changed into a woman. . . . The initiation ceremonies change boys into women, or, rather, manwomen."[58]

Roheim stresses the significance of the use of the term "milk" in the sacred songs to describe the blood derived from the penis. Comparing food taboos, he remarks on the similarity between those applying to men bleeding from subincision and those for menstruating women. In further support of his contention that the men are playing the part of menstruating women,[59] he quotes an Arunta, who stated that if a woman sees a man's blood flowing from the veins she must either be killed, or a large group of men must have intercourse with her. Roheim feels that they do this to reassert their manhood which is in danger if their ("menstrual") blood is seen by a woman.[60] Another parallel may be found in the stories of mythical women who used their menstrual blood to smear their ceremonial poles, just as men now use blood from the subincision wound for the same purpose.[61]

It may well be that the magical qualities generally ascribed to menstruation and menstrual blood account for its supposed use on the ceremonial poles in mythical times. But whenever a potent magic is to be invoked by these Australians, blood is used. The magical quality ascribed particularly to menstrual blood forms the basis of the theory of subincision put forth by Ashley-Montagu:

"The element common to all forms of subincision is the inevitable effusion of blood. . . . Briefly, the suggestion here is that male subincision or incision corresponds, or is intended to correspond, to female menstruation. Indeed, I may at once state the hypothesis which I am about to offer as an explanation of the probable origin of subincision in Australia; it is that subincision in the male was originally instituted in order to cause the male to resemble the female with respect to the occasional effusion of blood which is naturally characteristic of the female, and possibly also with respect to producing some feminization in the appearance of the male organ."[62]

While he recognizes that the purpose of subincision is to make men resemble women physiologically and anatomically, he thinks it is only "for the purpose of permitting the bad humours of the body, and such as are likely to be produced during the performance of certain tasks with which a great deal of power is associated, to be liberated and voided."[63] To my way of thinking, his analogy is not broad enough.

The appearance of menstrual bleeding indicates the ability to bear children; its temporary stoppage during pregnancy suggests a further link between menstruation and creating new life. Thus menstrual blood, or any blood drawn from the genitals, may seem a substance that has powerful influence over life. The Arunta believe it will restore endangered life, as in cases of sickness. While menstrual blood is supposed to restore power to the man, blood from the subincised penis is believed to have the same effect on woman. When menstrual blood is not available and a man is seriously ill, blood is drawn from the labia minora and one of the women takes a witchetty grub, dips it into the blood and gives it to the man to eat. Afterward his body is rubbed over with the blood. When an aboriginal woman is very sick, one of the sons of her youngers sisters draws blood from the subincision wound; she drinks part of it and he rubs the remainder over her body, adding a coating of red ochre and grease. In all cases of illness, the first remedy is to rub red ochre over the body.[64]

It could be readily understood if, in higher civilizations, and with the greater importance of men, the ritual of subincision were reduced to circumcision. Unfortunately, the available evidence does not show such an evolution. Ritual castration, the most extensive mutilation, occurs among relatively high civilizations and is not found among the most primitive. But its absence is understandable, since to relate the penis in any way with fertility, even negatively, calls for recognition of its role in procreation; and this understanding is found in the higher, not the lower civilizations. Anthropological data do not suggest that ritual circumcision developed later in history than subincision and the diffusion theory indicates that subincision developed considerably later.[65] Indeed, the fact that subincision generally follows circumcision in the sequence of rites suggests that circumcision is probably older.

Thus even the order of the two mutilations indicates that circumcision may have been a male substitute for the first menstruation of girls, and that subincision was a second effort to procreate, when the first attempt failed.

The Men-Women

UP TO NOW I have dealt mostly with initiation rites that include circumcision and subincision. But many initiations do not include either one. Moreover, many initiation rites—both among tribes that practice the two mutilations and those that do not—contain other elements that are most readily explained as a reenactment of childbirth.

Apart from altering his own body, man can try to emphasize his contribution to childbearing negatively or positively. Using the positive approach, he can claim directly or symbolically to give birth to men; this is the method used among tribes whose initiation behavior is discussed below. The negative way is to de-emphasize the importance of the woman's contribution (illustrated by the biblical promise of God to make of Abraham a great nation, with no mention of Sarah) or to become convinced that it is negligible (exemplified by the Pilagá; see page 131); or to attract attention away from the actual process of childbirth and toward the man, by such customs as the couvade.

In general, as Briffault has noted, the actual process of childbirth is ceremonially a rather inconspicuous event in many preliterate societies. Often the mother simply goes into the bush to be delivered, washes the newborn child, and then goes back to work.[1] Since Spencer and Gillen have little to say about childbirth or customs related to it, while they discuss at some length the belief that only men can find spirit children, we may infer that this matter-of-fact attitude prevailed among the Arunta, although Kaberry's report (see page 122) suggests there is a certain amount of related ceremony.

The Couvade

The custom of the couvade surrounds childbirth with an elaborate ritual, but a ritual of men, not of women. As it is practiced among one people, the couvade is described as follows:

"The woman works as usual up until a few hours before birth; she goes to the forest with some women, and there the birth takes place. In a few hours she is up and at work. . . . As soon as the child is born, the father takes to his hammock, and abstains from work, from meat and all food but weak gruel of cassava meal, from smoking, from washing himself, and above all, from touching weapons of any sort, and is nursed and cared for by all the women of the place. . . . This goes on for days, sometimes weeks."[2]

Briffault says that the purpose of the couvade is to stress the indissoluble relation between the husband and the wife's group which comes into being when a child is born to them.[3] One can understand why this occasion is chosen to celebrate the relation, but the purpose does not account for the specific means.

Malinowski explains the couvade somewhat similarly: "In the ideas, customs and social arrangements which refer to conception, pregnancy and childbirth the fact of maternity is culturally determined over and above its biological nature. Paternity is established in a symmetrical way by rules in which the father has partly to imitate the tabus, observances and rules of conduct traditionally imposed on the mother. . . . The function of couvade is the establishment of social paternity by the symbolic assimilation of the father to the mother."[4]

I agree with Malinowski that the couvade is a custom over and above the biological nature of maternity, since it reverses the biological roles. While it is a "sympathetic" association according to Briffault, the man who envies the woman's ability to bear children has no "sympathy" for her. She is expected if not compelled to resume her work immediately, though she is exhausted from labor and the physiological postpartum readjustments. The husband and father, on the other hand, rests. His empathy with the mother is so great that he recreates in himself the need for special care that would be appropriate to her and which he denies to her.

We may look to comparable types of behavior in our own society for help in understanding these actions. Many situations exist in which we observe such role playing, such "sympathetic" association; in which one person plays the role of another without regard to biological facts. Consider the small child who dresses up in his parent's clothing, copying paternal behavior. Here, too, is seen a denial of biological differences, a symbolic assimilation of an alien role. Functionally it seems a preparation of the child for his adult role, but that explanation does not answer the question of why the child wishes to prepare himself for the role or to assume it prematurely. What we learn by observing the child is that he play-acts the role of father or mother because he wishes to be in their place, or at least to be like them—and at once. He is not thinking of his future role in the family, nor does he wish to emphasize his "indissoluble relation" to his parents. He imitates his parent because he is envious of or strongly attracted by the importance, the power, and sexual privilege of the parent.

While the couvade may very well serve those ends ascribed to it by the functional anthropologists, psychologically it seems closer to what motivates the child in playing parent. The man wishes to find out how it feels to give birth, or he wishes to tell himself that he can. In the pretense, he tries to detract from the woman's importance; but like the child, he copies only the insignificant externals and not the essentials, which indeed he cannot duplicate. Such an apeing of superficials only emphasizes the more how much the real, essential powers are envied. Women, emotionally satisfied by having given birth and secure in their ability to produce life, can agree to the couvade; men need it to fill the emotional vacuum created by their inability to bear children.

Transvestism

The analogy of the child dressing up in his parent's clothes can be examined more literally in those rites in which donning the clothes of the other sex figure importantly. The Naven ceremony described by Bateson is a central rite of one New Guinea tribe where the general behavior of the men is extremely masculine. In the Naven rite they go further than most tribes in revealing their desire for the feminine. One outstanding feature is the exchange of clothing between the sexes, but in this case it is the sponsor, not the boy initiate, who dresses up in woman's attire. Specifically, he wears dirty widow's weeds and is referred to as "mother." The masquerade is not intended to deceive; everyone knows that he is a man acting like a woman. The wearing of widow's clothes suggests something further: that the novice has only one parent, a ritual "mother," and no father; and the mother is neither all male nor all female, but both. The ceremonial "mother" is also made to look pregnant, his abdomen being bound with string like that of a pregnant woman. Thus attired, he wanders about the village looking for his "child," inquiring for him in a high-pitched, cracked (female) voice.[5]

It is also common in initiation for the novice to wear clothes and adornments of the other sex. Eiselen speaks of the *boxwera* dress, a female garment the making and wearing of which is important in the rites of the Bamasemola boys.[6] Many similar examples are also found in Frazer. He reports, for instance, that East African boys, after circumcision, dress as women and continue this mode of dress until their wounds are healed, after which they are shaved and assume warriors' clothes. Among the Nandi, young girls give the boys their own clothes and ornaments, which the boys wear for several months before they are circumcised. As soon as the operation is over, they exchange the girls' clothing for the garments and necklaces of adult women, provided by their mothers; these garments they wear for months after circumcision.[7] Similarly, among the African Chaga, the boys who return from circumcision are given their mothers' clothes to wear and are addressed as *mpora,* a term generally used of young women.[8]

Nothing could emphasize more clearly the unconscious connection between the circumcision of boys and the change from girl into woman. It is as if, among the East Africans, the change from girls' to women's clothing is used by the boys according to the tradition to declare: Circumcision has changed us from nonmenstruating (sexually immature) persons into persons who can show their sexual abilities as clearly as women do by bearing children. That the boys receive girls' clothing from any girl, but women's clothes only from their mothers, may also signify that their mothers reward them for circumcision.

Frazer concludes that the custom of exchanging clothes during initiation rites has been "practiced from a variety of superstitious motives, among which the principle would seem to be the wish to please certain powerful spirits or to deceive others."[9] But who are these "powerful spirits," and why is it pleasing to them that one sex should dress in the garments of the other? And who is deceived, and what is the purpose of the deception? Who invented these spirits; that is, from whose unconscious do they spring? Are they the projections of the men, of the women, of the elders, or of the initiates? Or are they perhaps, in some measure, the projections of all of them?

Frazer and other authors report mostly of boys' wearing women's clothing, but transvestism in initiation is by no means restricted to the male sex. Hollis reports a parallel custom among Nandi girls who, three days before their circumcision, are dressed as warriors, and given a tobacco pouch (otherwise a male prerogative) and men's body ornaments.[10] Basuto women during the time of their initiation wear men's clothing, carry weapons and are very impertinent to the men.[11]

It is possible to see in these customs a ritualized last effort to enjoy a social and possibly also a sexual role other than the one prescribed by society and imposed by biology. Now, on the threshold of adulthood, boys and girls are given a last chance to play both sexual roles. In initiation the desire seems very strongly stated, perhaps because it is for the last time; afterward, each person must settle down permanently to the single behavior assigned to his sex.

Initiation as Rebirth

That initiation is a symbolic rebirth, usually with the male sponsors acting the part of those who give birth to the initiates, is now widely accepted. Again and again, in tribe after tribe, anthropologists report puberty rituals in which rebirth plays a prominent part. Among more sophisticated peoples, it is sometimes an abstract, symbolic drama. Among others it is a frank acting out of childbirth. As in all things related to initiation, there is infinite variation, but the following account may be taken as fairly representative:

"In the west of Ceram [one of the Indonesian islands] boys at puberty are admitted to the Kakian association. . . . The Kakian house is an oblong wooden shed, situated under the darkest trees in the depth of the forest, and is built to admit so little light that it is impossible to see what goes on in it. . . . Thither the boys . . . are conducted blindfold, followed by their parents and relations. . . . As soon as each boy has disappeared within the precincts, a dull chopping sound is heard, a fearful cry rings out, and a sword or spear, dripping with blood, is thrust through the roof of the shed. This is a token that the boy's head has been cut off, and that the devil has carried him away to the other world. . . . So at sight of the bloody sword the mothers weep and wail, crying that the devil has murdered their children. . . . During his stay in the Kakian house . . . the chief . . . warns the lads, under pain of death . . . never to reveal what has passed. . . . Meantime the mothers and sisters of the lads have gone home to weep and mourn. But in a day or two the men who acted as guardians or sponsors to the novices return to the village with the glad tidings that the devil,* at the intercession of the priests, has restored the lads to life. The men who bring this news come in a fainting state and daubed with mud, like messengers freshly arrived from the nether world. . . ."[12]

Or, one might say, like persons totally exhaused after childbirth. The boys know that they were not reborn and that the priest acted the role of the devil. Significant features of this ritual are also the wish to fool the women by pretending that strange and supernatural events take place, and the secret pact of the men never to reveal the truth to the women.

The dark, oblong hut may represent the womb to which the boys return to be reborn. That the ritual may be designed to imitate the act of parturition is also suggested by the behavior of the boys themselves, who afterwards pretend to be as disoriented as newborn infants. When they return to their homes, they act as if they had forgotten how to walk, tottering and entering the house backward. If food is given to them, they hold the plate upside down. "Their sponsors have to teach them all the common acts of life, as if they were new-born children," including how to talk.[13]

The elaborate ritual of the Liberian Poro society may be considered representative for a whole group of tribes which relegate circumcision to a minor role compared

---

* Devils and a nether world have little place in the mythology of these tribes; probably they are concepts introduced by white men, particularly missionaries, to whom we owe so many excellent observations on the lives of preliterate people. What they and some anthropologists call "devils" are more often than not viewed by the people they write of as deceased ancestors or mythical forefathers.

with the ceremony of rebirth. In general, one should beware of judging the relative importance of rites, but here we are told specifically that "circumcision was a minor rite," and the circumcised boy was considered an outsider until the "spirit had eaten him."[14] In this ritual the Poro deity, the crocodile spirit, swallows the boys who, on entering the ceremonial place, undergo a ritual death. During the time they are supposed to be in the crocodile's belly, they live away from home in the bush, a time extending up to four years. There they are scarified with the marks of the Poro, made by the teeth of the spirit when he swallows them. Since the crocodile spirit has swallowed the novices, he is "in a state of pregnancy, as it were, until the close of the [initiation] school's session, when those who are still alive are 'borne' by him."[15] Finally they return to town, pretending to be newborn and failing to recognize even their oldest and closest friends.[16]

While the boys are in the "womb" they lose their foreskins but incorporate part of the female genitalia. Since a number of boys really die during the initiation period, the idea that all have died and that most of them were reborne by the male spirit gains credence.

This ritual contains the interesting feature of the boys' being marked with the teeth of the Poro. It may be that fantasies of the so-called vagina dentata, not uncommon among neurotic and psychotic patients, are here combined with those of oral incorporation. The ritual markings of the Poro may then symbolize not only the swallowing of the boys but also their rebirth. Abraham's report on one of his male patients who likened the vagina to the jaws of a crocodile[17] indicates that modern Western men may produce similar spontaneous fantasies. If so, they suggest why the crocodile was chosen by the Liberians as the animal to rebear the initiates.

Since the male anxiety about the dangerous vagina is suggested, the scarifications may also symbolize mastery of the initiate's fear, his safe, perhaps victorious passage through the vagina dentata. Eating part of the female genitalia further suggests that he may also be mastering great fear of or desire for the vagina through oral incorporation.

I should add here that these tribes are familiar with the physiology of birth; hence even rebirth through the Poro cannot assure the men they have created life. So it may be that they replace mastery through acquisition (symbolic childbirth) and showing that they are not afraid. Such a change in behavior can be observed in children too. When they have shouted, "I'm stronger" or "I'm better" and it no longer works, they resort instead to "I'm not afraid of you" to indicate mastery.

Frazer, stressing the connection between initiation rites and birth and rebirth, says:

"Can it be that circumcision was originally intended to ensure the rebirth at some future time of the circumcised man? . . . The conjecture is confirmed by the observation that among the Akikuyu of British East Africa the ceremony of circumcision used to be regularly combined with a graphic pretence of rebirth enacted by the novice. If this should prove to be indeed the clue to the meaning of circumcision, it would be natural to look for an explanation of subincision along the same lines. Now we have seen that the blood of subincision is used both to strengthen relatives and to make water-lillies grow. . . . The intention of both ceremonies would thus be to ensure the future reincarnation of the individual. . . . That portion, whether the foreskin or the blood, was in a manner seed sown to grow up."[18]

Frazer emphasizes here the "strengthening and fertilizing virtue of the blood" which he thinks accounts for subincision, and even compares its power to that of a "seed sown to grow up." Although he uses these terms symbolically, the connotations the rites held for him are obvious. He also reports an initiation ceremony which he interprets as a pretense of conceiving the boys anew. The priests (acting as birth-giving fathers) smear their faces and bodies with water that has been dyed red and represents blood.[19] Frazer's interpretation is that they are bleeding from defloration, but to me the ceremony suggests that they are bleeding from childbirth.

Interpreting rituals on the basis of their possible symbolic meaning is hazardous, especially if the interpretation is based on experience in an alien culture. Still, the following ritual seems significant in its re-enactment of intrauterine existence and emergence at birth:

"When the [Nandi] boys have recovered [from circumcision] the *kapkiyai* ceremony is held. A pool is made in the river by means of a dam, and a small hut built in it. All strip, and, preceded by the senior [initiator], the boys crawl in procession four times through the hut. They are thus completely submerged by the water."

After this last ceremony of initiation "the boys may now go forth and see people, but they must still wear women's clothes."[20] Submersion in water is of course a common initiation ceremonial; in our own culture we have baptism. But in Nandi ritual, the immersion that so often symbolizes return to or emergence from the womb, and rebirth in general, is combined with another symbol of the uterus, the hut. In addition, the boys have to crawl, which means they approach the fetal position. Usually, the hut that appears in many initiation ceremonies can be disregarded as a maternal symbol; after all, the initiates must spend their time of seclusion somewhere, and the hut is an everyday habitation. In this case, however, the hut is literally in the water and thus directly related to immersion and the crawling position. The combination might thus be viewed as an effort to recreate the intra-uterine existence, where the infant is confined in a small, dark place and surrounded by fluid.

Among Australian tribes, where there is less subtlety and more direct action, where the secrecy of the male rites is not used to cover up lies told to women in order to overawe them, rebirth is not merely claimed but is acted out openly. In many details, the men treat the initiates as if they were babies to whom they had just given birth. For example, the men carry the boys on their shoulders as women carry their babies. They squat over the fire to allow smoke to enter the anal opening, thus performing the same healing and purifying rites that women undergo after childbirth. They even say that, in letting the smoke enter the anus, they do as the mythical Wawilak women did when they gave birth to a baby.[21]

During initiation ceremonies in New Guinea (which include scarification but not circumcision) the male sponsor behaves as a comforting "mother" to the novice. He holds the boy in his lap and consoles him while the incisions are made. When the boy screams, the "mother" will say, "Don't cry," holding him still and at the same time responding to his frantic clutches. After the scarification is finished, the sponsor carries the child on his back, as mothers do their babies, to the pond where the blood is washed off. Then he carries him back to the ceremonial house and applies soothing oil to the cuts.[22]

Arapesh initiation also stresses maternity symbolically. The sponsors cut their arms, mix the blood with coconut milk and feed it to the novices, who thus ceremonially become their children.[23] From these and other observations, Mead concludes that the cult assumes that boys can become men only by ritualizing birth; in this way they take over, symbolically and collectively, the functions that women perform individually and naturally.[24]

Experience with seriously disturbed and schizophrenic preadolescent children shows that the desire to be pregnant and to give birth is as common among boys as among girls, and that it is most acutely activated by a new pregnancy of the mother or a mother figure. Boys as well as girls may then imagine themselves to be pregnant; they may even overeat and manage to develop the protruding abdomen, the stance and gait of a woman in the later stages of pregnancy. Similarly, "hysterical" morning nausea in imaginary pregnancy can be found among boys as well as girls.

If we may again draw inferences from the unconscious of modern disturbed children to those of persons in less civilized societies—although it is an open question whether such inferences are valid—we may conclude that the start of the childbearing age in girls precipitates feelings in men similar to those that the mother's pregnancy rouses in schizophrenic children. Thus initiation rites come at adolescence, and the boy must be reborne by a man.

Much depends, of course, on the nature of the male-female relationship in the society. The psychological mechanism behind the assertion that rebirth takes place in initiation may in many cases be very simple: men's desire to detract from the importance of childbearing or to cancel their own obligations to women as the source of life.

Separation

Some authors stress that the purpose either of the total puberty rites or of the rebirth ceremony is to break the close ties the child has formed to the mother and to replace them with a stronger bond to men, since the men have now given life to the boys as their mothers did.

A wide variety of means is used to divorce the initiate from his past and to signify that new life begins at initiation. The Nandi novices are given purges and their heads are shaved; the Indians of Virginia gave the boys emetics to obliterate remembrance of the past; in South Africa, the Xosa boys discard their clothes and invert their speech[25] (just as the baby comes into the world with little or only very short hair, naked and without speech). The Damaras reckon a man's age from the date of circumcision, not counting the earlier years at all.[26] Another common custom is to give the initiates new names, a particularly significant act because of the intimate connection between a person and his name and because magical functions are often assigned to names. Laubscher reports that South African boys, for example, are given new names after circumcision and that these people believe implicitly that new life is attained as a result of the operation.[27]

Certain psychoanalytically oriented authors have gone further in stressing separation, claiming that the purpose of the ceremonies is to sever the Oedipal ties. Laubscher, for example, says that in order to pass from the childhood phase of female dominance into the second phase of male dominance and control the boy must experience a psychological rebirth into the world of men, severing all his attachments to the mother. Hence the usually rigid taboo prohibiting women from taking part in initiation.

It is certainly true that closely knit age groups are often formed around the shared experience of initiation. Among the Masai of East Africa all those initiated within the same quadrennium are linked for life, accepting many mutual obligations and claims.[28, 29] Clearly, strong emotional bonds must exist between the members of these age societies, based on the commonly experienced satisfaction of deep emotional needs at the time of their creation; that is, at initiation.

Modern parallels can be drawn between these initiatory groupings and spontaneous youth movements where scarification was as central an adolescent ritual as it is in initiation. German students were more than willing to suffer scarring and bloodletting, proudly considering the dueling ordeal as a proof of manliness and their right to belong to the group. Like the African age mates, these young men who attained manhood together were bound in fraternal "Corps" for life. Their student rituals simultaneously satisfied early sadistic and masochistic desires, while life in the fraternities offered some satisfaction to other pregenital and homosexual tendencies.

Other modern youth groups, though they may contain a strong homosexual element, often gain their cohesion from a common experience of satisfying more genital instinctual desires, as in shared sex experiences. Among middle-class adolescents it may be a group visit to a house of prostitution; or in lower-class gang life, successive intercourse of all members with a willing or unwilling female. Similarly, members of college fraternities are united by the shared introduction into adult life and its satisfactions.

Accepting this viewpoint, it becomes immaterial whether the actual arrangements for initiation rites are made by elders as prescribed by tradition, or whether they spring up spontaneously among adolescents. It might be an essential difference between a tradition-bound and a "free" society that in the first, rituals are established by the elders to provide for at least partial satisfaction of youth's inner needs, while in a so-called free society each generation must develop its own way of satisfying those needs.

The Australian tribes discussed so often in this book consist of small groups with little other than totemistic subgroupings. But in the social organization of other, more advanced tribes, age classes are often an important grouping or even, as among the African Chaga, the most important one.

One might even speculate as to whether men did not create the larger forms of society after they despaired of being able, by magic manipulation of their genitals, to bear children.*

Freud and many others (Blüher, for example[30]) thought that these larger forms of society were based on homosexual attachments. The lead taken by men in this area may thus have had its roots in associations that were first formed around initiation. In Central Australia, many tribal groups that otherwise live separated from each

* See also the earlier reference (page 56) to Chadwick's theory that it was men's disappointment at their inability to create human beings which led them to intellectual creation.

other come together at the close of initiation ceremonies, in what might be viewed as a larger societal organization. Spencer and Gillen describe in detail how on such occasions messengers are sent out, inviting the various groups to come together,[31] how they meet, and how at these meetings important decisions are made encompassing much larger groups than those the tribes ordinarily live in.

"It is, indeed, a time when the old men from all parts of the tribe come together and discuss matters. Councils of the elder men are held day by day, by which we do not mean that there is anything of a strictly formal nature, but that constantly groups of the elder men may be seen discussing matters of tribal interest; all the old traditions of the tribe are repeated and discussed, and it is by means of meetings such as this, that a knowledge of the unwritten history of the tribe and of its leading members is passed on from generation to generation."[32]

Even today, age groups that are based on initiation to the Poro society act as social units in later life, in peace and war. More important, the leaders of this society are those who administer justice, and it is their influence that binds the small Liberian tribes into larger units. "The function and influence of the Poro [society] . . . is felt even outside tribal limits, and many details of the organization are intertribal, so that a man of high standing will be so recognized even in a distant tribe whose language he cannot speak."[33]

Society may thus have been founded not on the association of homicidal brothers (postulated by Freud) but on a joint effort of men to master a common problem. This is not set forth as a new hypothesis on the origins of society. I merely want to indicate that theories entirely different from those current in psychoanalytic literature may be equally plausible.

The Secret of Men

IF THE BASIC PURPOSE of male initiation were to teach tribal lore or to ritualize maturity, it would be easy to see why it should be marked by elaborate ceremonies intended to give it special dignity and impressiveness. But if these were its only purposes, it is hard to find a plausible reason for its being shrouded in secrecy and forbidden to women and children. Tribal lore would be more effectively taught if every member of the community were instructed repeatedly, and from childhood. A deep impression can be made when the entire population takes part in or observes a ceremony, as in inaugurations or coronations. If secrecy is used for greater impressiveness there must be particular reasons that make secrecy more effective than wide public participation.

Sometimes the purpose of secrecy is to keep a magic power from the hands of unbelievers, or from enemies who may use it for sorcery. But in many cases it is intended to make those excluded think that initiates have superior powers.

The Original Secret

Accepting for the moment my interpretation of initiation rites, it may be inferred that the act of birth is kept as great a secret from men as the act of initiation is from women. This indeed appears to be the case. Among the Australian aborigines, little ceremonial secrecy accompanies first menstruation or the so-called initiation of women; but childbirth rituals are so secret that they evaded the attention of most observers.

It may also be that the androcentric bias of male observers was reinforced by the reluctance of aboriginal women to let any man learn of this, their greatest secret. In any case, we owe most of our knowledge of these rituals to women investigators, and even Kaberry reported that she found it harder to get an account of the childbirth songs from the women than to discuss initiation with men. She lived with the natives for seven months before she finally heard the first of these songs, although she had previously seen a women's secret corroboree.[1]

"Now although the men know some of the details of childbirth . . . still they are ignorant of those songs which are sacred . . . [and] which for all their simplicity are fraught with the power that they possess by virtue of their supernatural origin. In so far as they are commands which appear to achieve their result automatically, they may be considered magical; but their efficacy is attributed to the fact that they were first uttered by the female totemic ancestors. They have the same sanctions as the increase ceremonies, . . . the cult totems, subincision and circumcision."[2]

The extreme secrecy of male initiation rites and childbirth ritual therefore suggests that they may be parallel phenomena; the parallel between male and female initiation seems external and nonessential by comparison.

On the other hand, while men speak of the secret of women and mean their sex apparatus and functions, women do not make a similar association to the secret of men. They may even scoff at the very idea of men's secrets. Berndt, in discussing the origin of the Australian Kunapipi rites, refers to one of the myths that tells how originally the men "had nothing: no sacred objects, no sacred ceremonies, the women had everything."[3] So one day the men stole the women's sacred objects and took them back to their own camp. The mythical Wawilak sisters, on finding that their sacred objects had disappeared, decided that perhaps it was just as well the men had taken them, since men could now carry out most of the ritual for them while they busied themselves chiefly with raising families and collecting food.[4]

Or as one of Berndt's present-day informants told him: " 'But really we have been stealing what belongs to them (the women), for it is mostly all woman's business; and since it concerns them it belongs to them. Men have nothing to do really, except copulate, it belongs to the women. All that belonging to those *Wawilak,* the baby, the blood, the yelling, their dancing, all that concerns the women; but every time we have to trick them. Women can't see what men are doing, although it really is their own business, but we can see their side . . . in the beginning we had nothing, because men had been doing nothing; we took these things from the women.' "[5]

Summarizing the question of why men and not women now act out these fertility rites, Berndt concludes that women "know that the rituals are principally concerned with peculiarly feminine functions and that men are carrying out the more strenuous features of ceremonial life. 'These rituals,' said one informant, 'are just like a man copulating with a woman, he does all the hard working so that the women can carry out the really important business of childbirth.' This may be a one-sided attitude, but it does adequately express local native reasoning in this matter."[6]

I cannot accept the obvious rationalization as to the cause of the division of labor. I suggest that the main reason for the existence of the rites is the men's desire for an equally important "business."

The Need for Secrecy

Other rituals go beyond a mere simple assertion that men have significant secrets. They are found in cultures as diverse as the preliterate African and highly civilized Greek, and include the long series of rites claiming the rebirth of initiates by men. Rites that claim occurrences contrary to nature, but that cannot demonstrate those events, must be kept secret. Otherwise the participants cannot tell themselves that such events have in fact taken place. Moreover, secrecy protects the believer against the doubt of sceptics who are kept from collecting evidence that might destroy the belief. Since initiation rites serve purposes that can be achieved only in symbol but not in reality, its fictions must be hidden if the devotees are to enjoy the psychological benefits of symbolic achievement. Secrecy is thus necessary for the continuing satisfaction of the needs of the believers.

Among some peoples, women may be killed even today for observing these rites. The Poro society's method of dealing with a woman who spies on the men shows it is her ability to reveal the secrets to others, rather than her own presence or knowledge, that destroys the power of initiation. Such a woman is not necessarily killed; she is often permitted to live in the initiation hut and to observe the ceremonies freely. But once initiation is over, she must remain mute for the rest of her life. If she should ever break down and talk, even if only in a dream, she is immediately killed by a member of the society.[7]

My views are not new. Lowie, for example, has expressed them in regard to the secrecy of the bull-roarer,* the swinging of which accompanies the most sacred ceremonies of the Australians.[8] Women and children are taught to regard the curious buzzing noise of the bull-roarer as the voice of a spirit that presides over the ceremony. But one of the secrets revealed to initiates, with great emphasis on the necessity of hiding it from the women, is the true nature of the bull-roarer and how men came to possess it. (*See* Appendix)

The everyday behavior of children offers parallel observations that suggest further explanation of the nature of this secrecy. Children often claim to possess secret knowledge, just because they feel so lacking in knowledge. A child will boast of some special piece of information which he does not have or which is as commonplace as the whirling of a flat stick (like the bull-roarer). Under no circumstances will he reveal the secret, since its only purpose is to give him status in the eyes of another person. By inventing a secret language, for example, and using it in the presence of a parent or older sibling whom the child considers superior to himself, he tries to convince the other person as well as himself that he is not inferior since he has certain important abilities or knowledge.

Blackwood too thinks that the main purpose of the male secret societies is to hoodwink the women. The men do not hesitate to kill a few boys in order to convince the women that all have been killed and that men have brought some of them back to life. This parallels the myth of the bull-roarer in which they killed all the women to keep them from telling that the bull-roarer was stolen by men. The men even cut down groves of areca palms, although the areca nut is a highly prized delicacy, to show women the power and malignancy of the male ghosts who kill their sons.[9] Like the neurotic who will readily destroy important possessions to keep his unrealistic defenses intact, these men destroy the cherished

---

* The bull-roarer is made of a small, flat piece of wood or stone, carved or otherwise decorated with sacred designs. Through a hole in one end a string is passed; swung rapidly it makes a booming, humming noise. In many ceremonies bull-roarers are swung, and it is maintained that the noise so produced is the voice of certain spirits.

palm trees to impress the women more thoroughly with their power to create life.

Donning the *Upi*

The relation between the secret of menstruation (a real one to those who do not understand physiology) and the pretended secrets of men can also be shown. Blackwood, for example, has referred to the secrecy surrounding the boys' wearing of the *upi*, a tall, awkward and probably uncomfortable hat made of palm leaves, which conceals the hair. The *upi* is put on while the boy's hair is short, and he wears it until initiation, never taking it off in the presence of women until it is ceremonially removed. On its removal, the women suddenly discover the mysterious secret of men: they have long hair. The main purpose of the ceremony is to surprise the women with the length of the hair.[10]

The Buka have three initiation ceremonies, the first of which is the donning of the *upi*, and the second its removal. In girls, the growing of the breasts may precede menstruation by some time; likewise the boys put on the *upi*, in the seclusion of the bush at about the age of nine, and take it off several years later. The terms used to designate pubertal boys and girls emphasize this parallel. The girl is called "a female whose breasts are developing," while of the boy they say, "he goes to the bush," meaning he has withdrawn to put on the *upi*.

Since so little actually happens—in this instance, such an ordinary phenomenon as the hair's growth—it is particularly necessary to declare it a great secret and to ritualize it. Only in this way can they pretend that what happens to boys at puberty is as important as what happens to girls. The *upi*, ridiculous though it may look to the foreign observer, is probably, as Blackwood says, the most serious and important factor in the whole culture of this area. Its rules and taboos profoundly influence the people's daily life.[11]

A natural physiological process shared by men and women is here construed to have some special supernatural meaning. The growth of hair is a particularly suitable symbol because pubic hair signifies adult sexuality in both sexes, and, in women, is coincident with the onset of menstruation. Even to modern children, female pubic hair is a matter of great interest. Disturbed children express their envy and anxiety about the adult woman's vagina in angry remarks about the "hairy vagina"; in some severely disturbed boys it often seems an obsession. Perhaps the pubic hair, which is visible in boys but only an incidental sign of sexual maturity, is indirectly emphasized and ritualized to compensate for women's much more obvious signs.

According to the myths, the *upi,* too, originally belonged to women and not to men. But the legend of its origin goes a step further, connecting the *upi* and the breasts by making the former a reward for the suckling of children. The legend, current over the whole area, runs as follows:

"A woman was walking in the bush when she saw an *urar* (ghost, spirit of person long dead) wearing an *upi.* The woman looked at the *upi,* and liked it very much. She said to the *urar:* 'Oh, I like you, you are my man, you are a fine fellow.' Then the *urar* took his long breasts and gave them to the woman, took hers, which were very small, for himself. Before that, the men had big breasts and the women small ones, afterwards, it was as it is now. The woman said: 'I don't want these big breasts, I want your *upi.* If you will give it to me I will not give it to any one.' The *urar* said: 'I don't want to suckle a child. If you have a child you must put him to your own breasts and give him milk' Then he gave her the *upi.* She hid it in the bush. But one day a man caught her with it, and took it away from her. He said: 'You must not tell any of the other women about this.' The woman said: 'It belongs to me and to all the women.' Then the man killed the woman. He said: 'It will be a bad thing if she stays here and talks about this to all the other women. I shall take this thing and put it in the bush, it won't do for any more women to know about it.' So he took the *upi,* and ever since then it has belonged to the men, and no longer belongs to the women."[12]

This myth resembles those telling of the origin of the bull-roarer. The story seems everywhere the same: real power is openly displayed, and recognition of its possession is taken for granted. Pretended power has to be surrounded by secrecy and ritual; otherwise, the world will realize that not only does the emperor not wear very special clothes but, in fact, no clothes at all.

Stopping Up the Rectum

The Chaga men, in a society where the importance attached to menstrual blood is very great,[13] claim ascendancy over women by acquiring power over a bodily function that women cannot control. They maintain that during initiation the anus is stopped up permanently and that after that men retain their feces. To be "stopped up" is identical with acquiring the rights of an adult male. This stopping up of the anus is the central rite of initiation; the novices are told that the plug is the sign of manhood and that guarding its secret is their first duty. Thus:

" 'Don't emit wind in the presence of women and uninitiated youth. If you do, the tribal elders will slaughter your cows. Neither must you be surprised by women when you defecate. Always carry a stick with you, dig your feces in, and scratch about here and there pretending that you are digging for some charm. Then if a woman should observe you, she will seek there and find nothing. . . . If you suffer from looseness of the bowels, call on one of your age mates to take you to the men's house to look after you there, for if your bride gets to know about it, it means misery to you. If you dare to tell anybody of the secret of men, then your age group, the tribal elders and the chief will without mercy deprive you of all you own. For you will have disgraced your contemporaries, yea the very dead themselves. And it will be said that the secret of the men is a lie.' The novices were therefore trained openly in basing their manhood on a fiction."[14]

Until recently this fiction was carried through to its final conclusion, with the performance in which the plug was "removed." A group of men would gather at the home of an old man and slaughter a goat, tying bleeding pieces of meat around his thighs so that blood ran down and covered his legs. Then they would remove and hide the bloody meat and call his wife, entrusting the old man to her care. They explained to her kindly that her husband had had his plug removed for his sons' sake and that the bleeding started when the stitches were taken out. The woman should not be surprised that the old man would thereafter again find it necessary to defecate. It was his wife's duty to help the old man, if at any time he should fall and expose himself, so that the young men should not make fun of him.[15]

Such a puberty rite, like many others, seems a symbolic counterpart to menstruation. Girls at first menstruation "open" their vaginas, since every month something is discharged from that body opening. Men at puberty pretend to close an orifice from which a discharge took place up to then. In old age menstruation stops, and the vagina seems to become closed. In old men the closed orifice is opened and its discharge is resumed.

The parallel between menstruation and the setting of the plug is further suggested by the way men are taught to hide their feces and girls their menstrual blood. Girls are told to bury the blood to hide it from their fathers and brothers, because it is a sin to let them see it, just as men are advised to hide their feces from females. Roheim recognized that the secrecy surrounding the male rites seemed "like a simple inversion of the menstruation taboo, the men saying 'We are not allowed to see your bleeding so we shall not allow you to see ours.' "[16]

But the pretended stopping up of the anus has an additional meaning. It is not only connected with menstruation but also with pregnancy. Thus, the setting of the plug also imitates the stop in menstruation—that is, the first indication of pregnancy. The Chaga women, who are aware of what is going on, regard the men's behavior with amused tolerance. In their own initiation rites, the girls are told that the men defecate but keep it secret from the women, and they are admonished not to laugh. The women realize that actually the secret is theirs; they say that when a woman becomes pregnant her source of blood is stopped up and that this is the original plug.[17]

I am not alone in my view of these rites: Gutmann approached the problem from an entirely different viewpoint, but his intimate knowledge of Chaga lore and Chaga people led him to similar conclusions. He says:

"The careful exclusion of women [from participation in initiation], the presentation of the whole ceremony as a new birth, all this can be readily explained by the desire of the men to demonstrate their legal right over their progeny. This they try to achieve by demonstration that the care they have exercised to arouse fecundity and to make it secure, equals the accomplishment of the mother on the occasion of giving birth to a child who cannot yet realize his sex.

"The pretense of setting the *ngoso* [plug], for example, is justified by the Chaga because it was necessary in order to create and secure respect of the women [for the men]. Such interpretation seems not too far off from what may have been the true origin of the invention of the *ngoso*.

"If it is correct that the content of the initiation ceremonies is a reshaping of men so that they can procreate, and if this reshaping is experienced primarily as a rebirth, then it is suggestive to set in parallel the time of men's preparation for procreation with the time period which the infant spends in the mother's womb, namely nine months. The period of caretaking after circumcision lasts for two or three months. The stay in the [initiation] grove where the teaching takes place lasts six months. In this way nine months elapse from the beginning of the ceremonies until their end, the final setting of the plug. Undoubtedly the most important mark of pregnancy aroused their interest. Through it they designate pregnancy and say: *mak akufungje:* the woman closes herself up. The setting of the *ngoso* probably, therefore, originally was to represent the counterpart to this on the part of the men. Moreover, it should surpass the contribution of women so that even greater honors were given to men. In this way, it seems, these men arrived at the pretense of claiming that men on reaching sexual maturity are able to digest totally and can do without elimination."[18]*

The Piling Up of Secrets

Somewhere in the course of the historical development that leads from the type of society of the Australian aborigines to the more complex forms achieved by many African tribes, man began to understand better the male contribution to procreation. Briffault remarks that "although magic-religious obscenity is prevalent in lower cultures, phallic symbolism is characteristic of rather more advanced cultural phases."[20]

Up to that point the penis as formed by nature was not considered good enough by some peoples. It had to be manipulated or even operated on to become more accept-

* According to Gutmann, the last time the young boys to be initiated were taken to the grove for such a considerable time was in the middle of the nineteenth century.[19]

able. But among some of those who came to recognize the erect penis as the male organ of procreation, the phallus could not be admired and venerated enough. Then the envy of women and the tendency to overstress the male contribution may have combined in the belief that the semen is all-important and the female contribution to childbirth negligible. The Pilagá of South America, for example, believe that "the man's ejaculation projects a complete homunculus into the woman, and that it merely grows in her until it is big enough to come out."[21] Counterreactive overevaluation is also seen in the phallic religions; the prayer in which the Jewish man thanks God he was born a man and not a woman may be a modern remnant.

If this development took place, then somewhere in between may have come a stage where magic manipulation of the genitals was no longer enough. With cultural growth and a greater knowledge of procreation, symbolic bleeding may have become less and less satisfying as proof of the male contribution to the begetting of children. Men could no longer tell themselves that they, too, had something equal to the woman's power of menstruation and pregnancy.

It may have been at this time that initiation ceremonies began to grow more intricate and secret. Because men began to doubt that circumciscion and subincision had given them the desired magic power, they may have added new rites to the ceremonies, hoping that these would provide it. But when their redoubled efforts still ended in failure, women's power may have seemed still more awesome and mysterious. So men may have arranged for secrets of their own. In the relatively complex civilization of the Chaga this process is nearly conscious, since one of the main purposes of initiation rites is to teach the boys to pretend to all women that men do not defecate. As time progressed, initiation rites became more and more elaborate; rite was added to rite, myth to myth, and secret to secret. Among some tribes the rituals finally became so intricate that their complete performance required years.

With neurotics, it commonly happens that if a symptom does not accomplish its aim it becomes more and more complex. The person is guided by the hope that if only he can refine the symptom enough it will eventually achieve the goal it was invented for. In the same way, perhaps, the more men came to realize that initiation rites did not confer powers of procreation, the more they insisted that the rites did confer some secret power. By now there are many societies where the men cannot even define the mysterious powers they so vehemently claim to have gained at initiation.

Girls' Rites

THEORIES that connect circumcision with the father's demand for obedience from his sons are not easy to apply to female circumcision. Little girls did not threaten the father's possession of the mother as a sexual object. Probably they were even quite willing and ready to serve the father in their female capacity. Numerous African tribes that circumcise girls are or were polygamous, and in many of them, women and girls were totally subject to the will of the father. It is difficult to see any reason for trying to reduce their sexual desires by frightening them, since they had no freedom of choice; certainly the father's incestuous desire for his daughter was not curbed by circumcising her. And if he were motivated by such desire, why would he not always execute the operation himself instead of relegating it to women, as is so often the case? If, on the other hand, women were jealous of their daughters' sexual desires for their husbands, how did they expect that circumcision would restrain those desires? It is impossible for a threat such as that of total castration to accompany female circumcision.

Also, if restraint were the purpose, there should have been admonitions urging obedience, as is sometimes true of boys' circumcision; but these are mostly absent from girls' rituals. Nothing in the rites, or in the myths concerning them, indicates that any particular or significant teaching of sexual avoidances takes place. On the contrary, the teaching in some tribes is concerned with making sexual life more enjoyable. Apart from this kind of instruction, girls' initiation has even fewer teaching elements than boys'. A minor but significant exception exists among the Chaga, where the girls are taught that the men's secret is a fake; but this is a direct consequence of what the boys are taught in their initiation. There is no relation between this teaching and the girls' circumcision —neither in the time sequence nor through ritual or myth.[1]

Natural Timing

The one feature that almost universally differentiates the initiation ceremonies of girls and boys is their timing:

for boys it is arbitrary, for girls it depends on natural change. The thought may have occurred to the reader that it is not true that there are no physiological phenomena to indicate sexual maturity in males. Ejaculation of semen is such a sign. And among the Zulus "the *Tomba* ceremony marks a very important stage in the life of the individual, viz., the attainment of physical maturity." It occurs "when his first genital discharge takes place."[2] But basing initiation rites on first ejaculation presupposes knowledge of the connection between the semen and fertility, a knowledge most preliterate peoples do not have. And since their rites are generally older than their knowledge, such rites as the *Tomba* are rare even among people who now understand reproduction.

Mead has pointed out, as did the boys at the Orthogenic School, how, in spite of the gradual changing of the voice, the growth of body hair and eventually ejaculation, there seems no exact moment at which the boy can say, "Now I am a man." Therefore it is a function of male initiation to punctuate a growth sequence that is inherently unpunctuated.[3]

Some tribes, among them the African Luvale, use the fact that the physiological changes in males do not become dramatically visible on a specific day to explain why the initiation of girls is less rich in content than the boys'. They point out that no special preparation can be made since the determining factor is the unpredictable onset of first menstruation.[4] But this rational explanation cannot fully justify the paucity of ritual, since many tribes do take note of the girl's first menstruation, either as a signal for several months' seclusion or for special veneration of the girl.

Though the onset of menstruation is the commonest occasion of girls' initiation, it is not the only one. The Central African Cewa think that a girl is ripe for initiation when her breasts begin to form.[5] The Arunta celebrate both steps in the girl's physical development. First:

"To promote the growth of the breasts of a girl, the men assemble at the men's camp where they all join in . . . an exhortation to the breasts to grow. . . . At daylight one of them goes out and calls her to a spot close to the men's camp to which she comes accompanied by her mother. Here her body is rubbed all over with fat by [her mother's brothers] who then paint a series of straight lines of red ochre down her back and also down the center of her chest and stomach. A wide circle is painted around each nipple."[6]

The next major event in her sexual development is ritualized as follows:

"In the Arunta and Ilpirra tribes a girl at the first time of menstruation is taken by her mother to a spot close to . . . the women's camp, near to which no man ever goes. A fire is made and a camp formed by the mother, the girl being told to dig a hole about a foot or eighteen inches deep, over which she sits attended by her own and some other tribal mothers. . . . During the first two days she is supposed to sit over the hole without stirring away; after that she may be taken out by one or other of the old women hunting for food. When the flow ceases she is told to fill in the hole. She now becomes what is called *Wunpa*, returns to the women's camp, and shortly afterwards undergoes the rite of opening the vulva and is handed over to the man to whom she has been allotted."[7]

The girl remains *wunpa* until her breasts hang pendent, the form characteristic of native women who have borne children, after which she is called *arakutja*, the name for a fully mature woman.[8] Thus there are four main events in the initiation of an Australian aboriginal girl: the development and painting of the breasts, first menstruation, opening the vagina and childbirth—all of them clearly defined steps in her development toward maturity.

Male ceremonies, on the other hand, could be set arbitrarily and could theoretically include any number of rites. However, they too have four phases (described in the Appendix). These have been related to girls' rites by Spencer and Gillen:

"In regard to the initiation ceremonies of women it is clear that there are certain ceremonies which are evidently the equivalents of the initiation ceremonies concerned with the men. The first one takes place when the girl's breasts are rubbed with fat and red ochre, and the second when the operation of opening the vagina is performed. This is clearly regarded as the equivalent of subincision in the male. . . . The first ceremony may perhaps be regarded as the equivalent of the throwing up and painting of the boys, there being amongst the women no equivalents of the circumcision or Engwura of the men."[9]

I agree with the authors' comments on the two equivalents. I might add that while there is no obvious parallel between boys' circumcision and girls' rites at first menstruation, it too may be inferred from the sequence of events.

What Spencer and Gillen fail to emphasize, however, is the relation between the rites and the timing of physical change. It seems more plausible to me that boys' rites are equivalent to the natural changes in women, and girls' rites are equivalent to boys' rites. The many other ceremonies that accompany boys' initiation are for the most part for totemic increase in which men claim to further the procreation of animals; these seem to be absent from girls' initiation. Roth adds that girls do not receive new names as boys do; obviously there is no feeling that women need to be reborn at or after puberty in order to be able to procreate.

The Menstrual Taboo

Nevertheless, we cannot simply observe that female puberty, being very marked, is otherwise devoid of ceremony. Indeed, among the Cuna Indians the most significant ceremony of the whole tribe, more important even than rites of birth, marriage, or death, is the formal recognition of womanhood accorded to girls who begin to menstruate.[10] But this is the exception. Despite their envied fertility, girls are socially at a disadvantage, and like men, they also experience ambivalence about their own and the other sex. Hence we find among preliterate people, as among civilized, a wide range of attitudes toward women and the ceremonies accorded them.

It is my opinion that the puberty rites of girls are more affected by men's attitude toward menstruation than by the physiological event itself. I have already suggested that men's feelings are shaped partly by women's reaction. I should like here to make the complementary point: Girls cannot help being deeply impressed by men's awe of menstruation. If an event appears taboo and uncanny to one part of the population, soon the other part begins to wonder about it, even if they at first took it for granted. Eventually it may cease to matter who first reacted with awe.

In view of Freud's subtle analysis of some major taboos, it is regrettable that he paid so little attention to those of menstruation.[11] In elaborating the principles by which all taboos should be understood, he said:

"Taboos are very ancient prohibitions. . . . These prohibitions concerned actions for which there existed a strong desire. . . . The persistence of taboo teaches, however, one thing, namely, that the original pleasure to do the forbidden still continues among the taboo races. They therefore assume an *ambivalent attitude* toward their taboo prohibitions; in their unconscious they would like nothing better than to transgress them but they are also afraid to do it; they are afraid just because they would like to transgress."[12]

One might add that if men had not envied menstruation *per se* they would have grown envious because it was tabooed. Perhaps the simplest explanation is that women were either specially attractive sex objects or felt stronger sex desires during menstruation, but that men were frightened, probably by the general fear of any loss of blood. In reaction, they may have tried to cancel out their fear of the bleeding vagina by avoiding it. But I think another explanation might be equally correct. In discussing taboos further Freud continues: "The taboo ceremonial of kings is nominally an expression of the highest veneration and a means of guarding them; actually it is the punishment for their elevation, the revenge which their subjects take upon them."[13] It might be, then, that childbearing and menstruation were once viewed as so elevating women that men, out of envy, imposed unpleasant taboos.

Benedict mentions the Carrier Indians of British Columbia who, at the onset of menstruation, caused the girl to live for three or four years in complete seclusion in the wilderness, far from all beaten trails. She was considered a threat to anyone who so much as saw her; even her footsteps defiled a path or a river. She was herself in danger and a source of danger to everybody else.

In other tribes this attitude is countered by adoration, and the girl's first menstruation is a source of blessing.

"Among the Apaches I have seen the priests themselves bow on their knees before a row of solemn little girls to receive from them the blessing of their touch. All the babies and the old people come also of necessity to have illnesses removed from them. The adolescent girls are not segregated as sources of danger but court is paid to them as direct sources of supernatural blessing."[14]

Male ambivalence about menstruation has recently been discussed by Devereux, who feels that "The Menstruating Woman as a Witch is, in a sense, the central theme of the psychoanalytic approach to menstruation,"[15] and that equally important positive feelings are ignored.

In a footnote, Devereux observes that even in some modern folk cultures the menstruating woman attains special dignity, if not veneration. While Italian peasants ascribe nefarious powers to menstruating women, they also believe that at the time of her monthly period she rises a notch in the social hierarchy; the peasant woman becomes a lady, the latter a noblewoman, the noblewoman a queen, while the queen becomes identified with the Madonna—in fact, menstruation specifically proclaims woman's kinship with the Madonna.[16]

He concludes that it is wrong to interpret the secluding of menstruating women as a sign of temporary degradation; on the contrary, he feels that the innumerable restrictions placed upon women and slaves clearly indicate where genuine power rests: in women, who propagate the species, and in the masses, who are the species.[17]

Mutilation of Girls

The term "female circumcision" is a misnomer, and in using it I have merely followed prevailing practice. It is characteristic that even for such a far-reaching mutilation of girls a term is borrowed that may really be applied only to boys. Female "circumcision" varies from tribe to tribe —it may be merely an incision of the hymen, or it may be extirpation of the clitoris or of the labia minora, or both. I have used the term "circumcision" when speaking of these varied operations, but it should be borne in mind that in the female it is not strictly a circumcision.

Roth describes the introcision of girls as follows: ". . . Two or three men manage to get the young woman, when thus ripe enough, all alone by herself away in the bush, and, throwing her down, one of them forcibly enlarges the vaginal orifice by tearing it downwards with the first three fingers wound round and round with oppossum-string."[18]

He feels that male subincision and female introcision are so analogous in essence, though not in appearance, that he prefers to use the term "introcision" for boys too.[19]

Berndt was impressed by another parallel: the one between subincision and the ritual defloration of girls:

"Young girls have their hymens pierced prior to intercourse on the ceremonial ground; others, whose hymens have already been broken through normal premarital coitus, have the end of the boomerang placed symbolically in the vagina. In the Rose River region, this form of defloration is a counterpart of the subincision rite."[20]

Roth also notes that female introcision is practiced only where male introcision occurs, and Mathew comments that wherever "subincision is practiced vaginal introcision becomes inevitable."[21] Kaberry, however, reports a contradictory case: the Lunga, though they do not practice introcision and deny that they ever did in the past, do perform subincision.[22] Thus the connection between the two rites in Australia, though general, is not inevitable. In other parts of the world, it cannot be found. Among African tribes that practice male circumcision but not subincision, varied mutilations of female sex organs are common. Obviously, there is no direct causal connection. Both mutilations may be caused by the same psychological tendencies, but speculation can go no further.

As for extirpation of the clitoris or the labia minora or both, it is not easy to understand what positive satisfactions are gained or who receives them. Psychoanalysts have suggested that the purpose of removing the clitoris is to eliminate clitoridean sexuality and to force women to enjoy only vaginal sexuality. This explanation has been accepted by a number of psychoanalytically oriented authors including Bryk. He thinks that by excision of the clitoris the Nandi girl's sexual freedom is curbed, and she is changed from common to private property, the property of her husband alone. That is, excision removes the organ most easily stimulated, and thus reduces the girl's sexual desires. Only in this way, he thinks, can she be forced into monogamy, which is contrary to her nature.[23] Such a theory conforms to the notion of the dual nature of female sexuality, which supposedly consists of an earlier phallic clitoridean, and a later genital vaginal sexuality. This theory, incidentally, rests on very shaky physiological foundations.

But even if the theory were more valid than I think it to

be, it would still not explain why the clitoris is removed. It would explain that only if one presupposed two things: First, that primitive men are consciously or unconsciously aware of the two types of sexuality in women, a condition we ourselves are by no means certain exists, and an awareness we cannot assume from what we know of these tribes or from their statements. Second, one would have to presuppose that the operation really has, or is supposed to have, some measure of success. But no vaginal sexuality is claimed by any of the people who practice excision of the clitoris.

This problem has been best discussed from a psychoanalytic viewpoint by Bonaparte. She suggests that Bryk actually derived his explanation from Freud, who, she says, seemed to agree with it. To this Bonaparte strongly objects: "I am inclined to think that the physical intimidation of the girl's sexuality through the cruel excision is probably no more able to feminize them, to vaginalize them, than the psychic intimidation of clitoridic masturbation imposed on little European girls."[24]

Bonaparte feels that both excision of the girl and circumcision of the boy result from the fathers' wish to "intimidate the sexuality" of the young. But such a desire is hard to understand, unless we assume that the father looks upon the girl's sexuality as promising pleasure to young males and resents the prospect. Bonaparte also refers to the desire of some men to find nothing masculine in the woman. They feel threatened by what seems phallic in women and hence insist that the clitoris be removed. Other men, remaining fixed upon the "phallic mother" of the infantile imagination, like to find something male in the woman. They include the men of those African tribes who wish to see the labia minora and the clitoris elongated until they somewhat resemble male genitals.*

Yet, as Bonaparte remarks, all these customs seem to satisfy only the imaginations of those who impose them. It is not likely that the girl's sexual nature is much changed. If the labia minora of the Bantu girls were extended to a quarter of a yard, they would still not constitute male genitals. Excising a woman's clitoris does not vaginalize her sexuality, nor does it make the muti-

---

* There is little or no evidence that men imposed on women the extension of the labia and clitoris. On the contrary, it seems to result from female desires.

lated woman less of a threat to the man who fears for his virility.[25]

Though we know that boys wish for circumcision from the statements of preliterate people, and from fantasies such as those reported by Nunberg, no such evidence has been gathered from girls. While the girl's anxiety about mutilation of the genitals is well known, even in my observations of schizophrenic girls I have only very rarely encountered a desire for such mutilation. In reviewing the literature one receives the impression that female introcision and excision are imposed on the girl by men. It is desired by her, if at all, not because it changes her sex organs but only because it brings higher status or is a necessary precondition of marriage.

Girls undoubtedly suffer from penis envy, as boys do from vagina envy; but while the evidence presented here suggests that boys try to satisfy their envy symbolically, it cannot be shown that the girl's parallel desires are satisfied by initiation as such. Dressing up in men's finery suggests mainly an acting out of envy for the male's role in society, but there seems no connection between this and any surgery on the genitals. The girls are not told, nor do they believe, that they gain new functions as a result of mutilation.

If it were true that by circumcision and subincision men tried and failed to match women's fertility, then it would be easy to see how they might grow resentful and try to revenge themselves on women. Men who tried to manipulate their penes surgically may have found it particularly offensive that women should possess a penislike organ in addition to female genitals; hence, they may have wished to take it away from women. A remark quoted by Bryk suggests such an attitude. When he asked one village chief of the Nandi about the custom of clitoridectomy he received the following answer: " 'We are Nandi. We don't want such a hanging down thing in our women!' In saying this, with his little finger he made an expressive movement as if to signify with it the clitoris and his disgust of it."[26]

But revenge, while perhaps a contributing factor, is probably not a major motive behind the mutilation of girls. I believe that the custom originates in more positive desires.

The Positive in Girls' Rites

Throughout this book I have been guided by the belief that important human enterprises, and certainly those that have given satisfaction for centuries, must serve positive rather than negative ends. This point of view conforms with ego psychology, which is just as concerned with the normal as the abnormal person and his motivations, while psychology of the unconscious was based mainly on the study of abnormal persons.

The neurotic may pray to God to mitigate His ire and rely on God to provide him with progeny and to protect him from sickness. The more adequate person will pray for positive guidance and then rely on his own ability to create new life, to develop hygiene and medicine in order to prevent and cure disease and to strive for better living conditions. The neurotic may cut off his nose to spite his face, but the normal human being, when for valid reasons dissatisfied with his nose, will submit to plastic surgery to improve his appearance.

I am unwilling and unable to believe that female rites were devised and kept up for centuries simply to provide women with rituals like men's or to wreak men's revenge on the female genitalia. Though a cherished toy may get broken when the small child angrily throws it away because it is too complicated or does not satisfy his desires at the moment, he does not break it only for revenge. His destruction of complex toys usually results from the effort to understand them, to learn how they work, to make them work as he wants them to; in short, to gain mastery over them. The more intriguing the toy, the greater the desire to control it and also to retain it. Any child gains some sense of mastery over the toy he can make run.

If I may make the analogy to female mutilations, it is possible to consider them as male efforts to gain control over female sex functions. After all, these people do not, like some neurotic children, destroy the cherished toy just because they cannot "run" it. The male is satisfied with a token command over the external female genitals that does not interfere with the woman's fertility or her sex enjoyment.

Female introcision as practiced by the Australians might represent an effort of men to make women bleed as in menstruation. The menstrual taboo is another, less direct assertion of male mastery; in this case, not over women's functions, but over their behavior when these functions occur. By chanting and rubbing the pubescent girl's breasts, the men can believe that they influence the development of the breasts. By all these acts men try to convince themselves and the women of their own positive contributions to fertility.

Female initiation rites devised or imposed by women, such as extension of the clitoris and labia, certainly provide the chance for socially approved masturbation; it may also be the result of women's desire to have a penis-like organ. Dressing like men, wearing men's ornaments and weapon's, etc., may help to satisfy their envy of men's social functions.

Some examples may illustrate the procedures that give women a greater degree of clitoridean or "phallic" sexuality than nature grants them, as well as a penislike organ. But the point to be emphasized here is that women adopt these practices without any encouragement or interference from men; hence the motivation must lie in the desires of women. In Dahomey:

"Girls who are from nine to eleven years old—that is, whose breasts are beginning to develop—are assembled by compounds in groups . . . and engage in the practice . . . of massaging and enlarging the lips of the vagina. They gather in the evenings at sundown behind the house of the woman in whose care they have been placed. . . . With a shaped piece of wood, this woman manipulates the lips of the vagina of each girl, pulling at them, stretching them, and lightly puncturing the vaginal tissues in several places. This she does eight to nine times for each of her charges during the first year of instruction, and during the next year the girls do this for each other. . . . For two years at the very least this is continued, and in addition there is the outer massaging of these 'lips' to cause thickening and muscular development for 'thin-lipped' women are considered lacking in comeliness."[27]

The African Luvale girl "is taught how to give sexual satisfaction . . . and there is no doubt that this is one of the most marked aspects of the instruction. . . . She also learns to make dancing movements with her hips during coitus. . . . In the unusual event of her being a virgin, her hymen will be broken with a stick or a piece of cassava root carved to resemble a penis. Her labia are also stretched. . . ."[28]

According to another account:

"The Maxi people use a horn [for enlarging and developing the lips of the vagina], though in Abomey both a special wooden instrument and the root of the indigo plant are employed, and, in addition, ants . . . the purpose of the introduction of this vegetable irritant or the stinging ants is to stimulate the process of massage, by inducing irritation which encourages tugging and handling. The [female] teacher, besides supervising this process, . . . also gives the girls instructions bearing on sexual life."[29]

Among the Baganda and the Suaheli the girl, before she reaches puberty, is encouraged to enlarge her labia through frequently pulling and stroking and by use of some special herbs or leaves.[30]

Such practices bring about changes of the genitals that can be connected neither with the teaching of tribal lore nor with wishes to bind the tribe together; they have no relation to *rites de passage,* nor to securing the incest taboo or inhibiting sexuality. They obviously increase the desire and opportunity for masturbation and, according to the teaching connected with them, enhance sex enjoyment for both men and women. Each is an age-grading experience that prepares girls for their future sex role and seems well in line with what girls of that age desire. It is not imposed by elders against the wishes of the young and serves hardly any other purpose than to provide sexual stimulation and to help the girls toward sexual maturity. Compared with such progressive experience, the female rituals that seem to be mainly copies of the male rites are lacking in conviction.

One last thought: the initiation of both boys and girls is probably modified by the ambivalence adults feel when confronted with young persons growing to maturity. On the one hand the adult is proud of the results of his training; but he may also envy the young who will soon replace him in positions of importance.

Such ambivalence may help to explain some, but only some, of the milder punitive and painful experiences that are inflicted on initiates, both boys and girls, that range from beatings to stinging by ants, wasps, or other insects, piercing parts of the body restricting movement, food, or rest, and so on *ad infinitum*. Bonaparte comments on how happy the old women must be who are delegated to mutilate the girls at this opportunity to take revenge on the young for their old age.[31]

I cannot agree that parents in any society are so forcefully jealous of their offspring. Their feelings are indeed ambivalent, but in the vast majority of cases the positive feelings are far stronger than the negative.

Parents who have loved their child and cared for him devotedly do not suddenly at the child's adolescence begin to act out wildly their minor negative feelings. What psychoanalytic reasoning may indicate, however, is that the older generation's envy of the young is in close ratio to the extent of its sexual frustration.

Thus the civilized, sex-inhibiting society may create much greater envy in parents than do those societies where the older people have enjoyed sexual satisfaction and continue to enjoy it as much as they wish to or are able.

Summary

The writer on female initiation finds relatively little material to work on. Partly because most investigators have been men, and partly because male rites are more prominent, the literature on female initiation is thin. But, on one point, female rites offer better evidence than male. In the myths explaining boys' rituals it is said that manipulation of the male genital was once performed by women; but in present practice the actual interference is nearly always performed by men. In the manipulation of the female sex organs, on the other hand, certain rites were and are performed by men and certain others by women. Thus in girls' rites we may find a clue to which types of manipulation are imposed by the other sex (and possibly why) and which are self-chosen or suggested and imposed by persons of the same sex on each other.

Comparing manipulation of the female sex apparatus by men and by women, it can be seen that, by and large, manipulation by men is destructive, showing an aggressive enmity that is most readily explained by fear or envy. Manipulation by women, on the other hand, results more often than not in greater sex enjoyment and in an extension of the sex apparatus that makes the existing organs more like those of men. That the labia, as Herskovits points out, become by artificial manipulation more muscular, harder, less flexible, is to make them more like the erect penis.

These practices, no less than the rites of boys, suggest again that the human being's envy of the other sex leads to the desire to acquire similar organs, and to gain power and control over the genitals of the other sex.

The Biological Antithesis

AT THE END of this study, I am still unable to explain circumcision fully and unequivocally. There is much evidence that women impose or desire it; but there is also much reason to believe it is desired by men—either because it gives them symbolically the capabilities of women, or because it emphasizes their masculinity by making the glans permanently more visible, or for a combination of these and other reasons. In any case all the explanations that appear most plausible to me seem to originate in the great biological antithesis that creates envy and attraction between the two sexes.

True, social differences in the status and prerogatives of the sexes compound the envy, including the greater sexual freedoms which may be accorded one over the other. In this last respect particularly, woman is still at a disadvantage. Yet even there, and still more so in regard to social status and role, our own society seems fortunately headed toward greater equality.

But in regard to what counts most, nature *permits* each person only one sex. Hence a desire for the bodily characteristics and functions of the other leads to a psychological impasse: to become like the other sex (which is desired) implies giving up one's own sex (which is feared). This impasse has been little recognized as a conditioning factor in so-called castration anxiety. That the anxiety reaches more deeply than parental influence can account for was recognized by Freud. So he looked to racial memory traces for its cause and concluded that we are born with a fear of losing our sex organs. I believe, instead, that our desire for the characteristics of the other sex is a necessary consequence of the sex differences. Fulfillment of that desire would imply losing our own genitals—hence the inexorable nature of castration anxiety in both sexes.

The efforts that I believe men and women make in most of the puberty rites discussed in this book are aimed at an actual or symbolic understanding of the functions of the other sex and a psychological mastery of the emotions they arouse. These efforts gain their impetus from the desire to master the riddle of our dual sexuality. Far from creating castration anxiety, they go a long way to conquer it. Hence we may come to view the rites as devised not to create sexual anxiety, but to control or eliminate it. If this is true, it will no longer seem so important to know what rites originated with men and what with women.

Up to now initiation rites, particularly circumcision, have been viewed by anthropologists and psychoanalysts as imposed mainly by elders on the unwilling young. But the schizophrenic children I observed developed something akin to initiation customs out of their deep inner needs. Neurotic or psychotic as their efforts may have been, they were clearly trying to help themselves. This led me to wonder if we had not taken too low a measure of man when we interpreted one of the greatest of his rituals as merely imposed by tradition or the hatred of his elders. I became more and more convinced that these rites are motivated not by a desire to break man's autonomy, or to prevent his self-realization as a person and a member of his social group, but by exactly the opposite desire. I believe the rites have little to do with any manmade conflict between the old and the young, or with securing the incest taboo or with an adherence to tradition. I believe instead that they are efforts to master the conflicts arising from man's instinctual polyvalent desires; also the conflict between such desires and the role society expects him to play.

There are many ways of dealing with a desire that is socially unacceptable or that for one reason or another the person himself cannot accept. One way is for the individual to dramatize it, act it out, and, through intense but in the long run only token satisfaction, try to rout it forever. Another way, still on the personal level, is to deny its existence by overemphasizing what is *not* unacceptable.

Society, too, may by rituals or institutions try either to help or to force the young person to deal with the problem. Some societies try to rid the person of tendencies ascribed to the other sex, so that he will act and feel as if these tendencies no longer exist in him. This solution is seen among people whose initiation rites stress only (or mainly) the manliness of boys and the womanliness of girls. Many of the better known demands made on pubertal boys and girls seem to exemplify this method. The feats a boy must perform to prove his manhood—such as killing an enemy among headhunters or playing football in our society—may well originate in the wish to deny what are looked on as feminine tendencies by overasserting his masculinity. Assertion of the female role in society is implied in such ritual acts as the girl's carrying a miniature house on her shoulders, symbolizing her position as the pillar of the home.[1]

While these rituals are usually considered a demonstration of what is manly or womanly, they are perhaps more correctly understood in their negative meaning, their denial of tendencies, that are supposed to belong only to children or only to adults of the other sex. Such tendencies include fearfulness in boys, and in girls a reluctance to being worn down by feminine tasks.

Another solution is seen in the pubertal *Nozhizho* rite of the Omaha Indians. The most important element of this rite is the adolescent's dream of the moon in which he may see a burden strap or a bundle of arrows held out to him. If in his dream he receives the burden strap, the emblem of a woman's life, he must thenceforth, regardless of the fact that he is a boy, live as a woman, use woman's language and dress. The girl who dreams that arrows are held out to her must, from that time forth, live as a man.[2] This would seem an admirable solution if the ways of life of men and women were equal in status and the social respect accorded them *and* if the decision were less absolute. That is, if it did not have to be made once and for all, but could be temporary or tentative, and of varying intensity or commitment to the ways of the other sex.

Still another way to minimize the conflict is to make it possible for the young person to satisfy at least part of his masculine and feminine strivings for the rest of his life. This seems to be the solution in societies that go furthest in equipping men with the semblance of female sexuality. What seems undesirable is that there is no going back. No allowance is made for individual variations in timing, intensity, or duration.

Our own social institutions provide all too few opportunities for either private or ritual integration of such desires. With our many masculine prerogatives, the girl's wish that she were also a man may be stronger or more open than the boy's wish that he were also a woman. Letting girls wear blue jeans is a poor and insufficient solution. In preliterate society, with its concentration on animal and human procreation, men's desire for a larger part in procreation may have been more pressing. Or it may be that in our masculine-oriented society, boys are forced by the mores to repress their feminine strivings more strongly than are girls.

For example, the importance of various forms of non-coital sexual activities can hardly be overstressed. Even sexual envy, though essentially irresolvable, could be mitigated if the mores, and hence their own conscience and self-respect, allowed men and women to play both the more active and the more yielding role as their emotions required at the moment—and not only in their social, but also in their sexual relations. Here, the psychoanalytic nomenclature, if not also the attitudes that account for it, is rather unfortunate. According to psychoanalytic theory, these sexual activities derive from what Freud called the polymorphous-perverse tendencies of the child and are to be satisfied in adults, if at all, through forepleasure. Though Freud viewed these concepts as value free, the term perverse, in common usage, has a negative connotation, while forepleasure connotes an activity with little merit in its own right. I find Jung's concepts and terms much more to my liking. He suggested that the child's sexual predispositions should not be viewed as polymorphous-perverse but rather as polyvalent, and remarked that "even in adult life the vestiges of infantile sexuality are the seeds of vital spiritual functions."[3]

This is certainly so, but polyvalent tendencies are also the seeds of social and sexual behavior, seeds which our society is only beginning to permit to be cultivated and to bear fruit in social and sexual practices. Of course, if these sexual activities are engaged in with guilt feelings because of social opprobrium or the individual's rejection of his own desires, little good can result, nor will they do much to mitigate the biological antithesis. In and by themselves they can only offer relief if they are part of a satisfying sexual relation between man and woman. Within a relation based on equal social and sexual rights and responsibilities, and accepted as part of such a relation, the satisfaction of polyvalent tendencies would go a long way to lessen the negative effects of the antithesis between the sexes. I am speaking, for example, of the male's desire to enjoy sexual yielding (also, and at times), and the woman's desire to enjoy sexual aggressiveness (also, and at times). And this, without the man viewing himself or being viewed by his partner as a weakling or as unmanly and the woman without viewing herself or being viewed by her partner as a virago.

At present, hardly any of our rituals permit youngsters or adults to dramatize or partially satisfy these desires. I would certainly favor, in a free society such as ours aspires to be, that solutions be found not in ritual but in personal ways that are respected by society. But as long as we do not offer any acceptable solutions to the problem, we should at least be more understanding and make allowance for it. If we could give greater recognition to boys' desire to bear children, to the desire of male adolescents and adult men for the more passive and leisurely enjoyment of life instead of having always "to fight and to strut," our boys and men might feel less envy and anxious hostility toward girls and women. They might also feel less need to compensate by keeping their emotional distance from women and by aggressive competing with one another. The freer men are to acknowledge their positive wish to create life, and to emphasize their contribution to it, the less need will they have to assert power through destructive inventions.

What needs to be satisfied is the desire of both men and women to play a significant part in the duties, obligations and prerogatives, the activities and enjoyments that in our society happen to be thought of as belonging to the other sex. This would permit them to find happiness, and thus self-realization, despite the biological difference of the sexes and despite the envy that is a "natural consequence." Each sex could then achieve greater inner autonomy, could better accept its own role and that of the other, and the two sexes could live with one another in a more satisfying way. In preliterate society men tried to solve this problem through ritual, it seems. We should be equally serious in our own efforts. What we might well search for are solutions that are more rational; solutions that, in line with the ethos of a free society, are more personal, more socially effective and more satisfying in private.

Infant Circumcision

THE PART PLAYED by circumcision in the Jewish religion, as well as the character of the God who demanded it, have been cited repeatedly as evidence that the deeper meaning of circumcision is submission to powerful father figures. Closer examination, however, reveals that the psychological influence, and indeed the motivation of circumcision, may have been very different before the advent of monotheism.

Sherman stresses that Jewish circumcision is a special case, characterized by three features unknown to other forms of the custom. They are: "(1) its marked religious significance; (2) the early age at which the operation is performed; (3) the absence of all trace of a female mutilation."[1] We may interpret these differences as indicating that in Jewish custom (1) circumcision became the mark of bondage to an overpowering father god; (2) that it was shifted from puberty (the age of sex assertion) to infancy (the age of utter dependence); and (3) that it became a purely male rite. Perhaps it was only by virtue of the changes in timing and sex selection, but primarily by the timing, that circumcision could become the vehicle of what Freud conceived of as castration anxiety.

I have already spoken in the text of the importance of two factors that shape emotional reactions to physical trauma. One is the psychological "constellation" within which the trauma is experienced; the second is the age (or the stage of psycho-biological development) at which the trauma occurs.

In the Jewish religion, circumcision occurs not at the age of greatest sexual vigor and self-assertion—which adolescence often is—but at the age of total dependence on parental figures. Thus it can become the symbol of "the covenant." The covenant confers special privileges, as does pubertal initiation, but, taking place at the beginning of life, it is not experienced as a change in status. The privileges to come hence seem as if they always existed. Moreover, while pubertal initiation makes the child a man, the Jewish covenant makes him forever a child whom the Lord will take care of provided he obeys His commandments. It is thus an agreement by which men give up their independence to a superfather who promises in return to look after them.

Such a ready relinquishment of independence because of anxiety is quite consistent with the helplessness of the infant. It is much less consistent with the tendencies of the adolescent who insists on self-determination, often in the face of great anxiety, and who defensively declares his independence from father figures.

When the child becomes older and learns about the circumcision that was inflicted in infancy, he may come to fear additional punishments from the father. Thus circumcision may lead to castration anxiety in particular or to the general fear of the true father or to the fear of the father figure which characterizes the Jewish religion.

The shift of circumcision to infancy may thus have been one step in establishing a paternalistic monotheism. The absence of female initiation among the Jews suggests another step: A custom that may once have promised individual independence and sex fulfillment to both sexes may have been arrogated in its powerful and magical function (entering the covenant with the Lord) to men alone. Excluding females from the rite indicates again how Jewish circumcision came to be linked with the castration complex. The main purpose of a circumcision inflicted on both sexes alike cannot be to curb incestuous desire in the male only. But circumcision of the male child alone, and in infancy, can have these consequences, since he remains for years afterward in the power of the father.

It is reasonable to assume that early monotheism, which had to fight for its existence, was particularly stringent in its superego demands just because it was surrounded by societies granting greater instinctual satisfactions. Perhaps the strictest, most castrating father god belongs precisely to the earliest monotheism; perhaps castration anxiety was evoked as a new weapon to keep man under his control. Assuming this to be the case, we are on the wrong track in examining Jewish circumcision for the light it may throw on circumcision in preliterate society.

The God of the Old Testament is perhaps the most rigorous of all superego images. Can we properly compare a feature of that monotheism with circumcision in a society where perhaps no clear separation had yet taken place between conscious and unconscious, in which id, ego and superego were probably less distinct from one another?

The use made by the Jews of the rite of circumcision may be compared with the Christian utilization of pagan customs; the rite was taken over but connected with entirely different myths. According to Freud, the Egyptian Moses imposed his religion on the rather primitive Jewish tribe. Whether or not this was so, it is possible that the custom of circumcision was diffused from Egypt to the Jews. Was it then that circumcision was assigned an entirely different meaning? A monotheistic religion whose chief tenet is subservience to an all-powerful god will have no use for rites that bestow great magic power on the individual as initiation did. The goals of such a reformer as Moses—whether he was Jewish or Egyptian— could be served best by retaining the ritual with all its power over the minds of believers and then, as in a reaction formation, attaching it to a myth that reversed its meaning.

Circumcision, which was a tool of man's greatest pride, may then have become the means of degrading him to the status of a helpless subject. Or to put it differently: the energy once used by the id to gain magic power through the manipulation of the genital was wrested away from the id. That energy was then claimed by an externalized superego which used it to restrain the id and to weaken the ego by making them subservient to a superego image.

If so basic a custom as initiation into adult life has retained for us not only the same form (circumcision) but also the same meaning as it had among preliterate people, one might ask how is it that we have reached a higher stage of civilization than they have? It is widely accepted that the external form of a ritual may persist relatively unchanged for long periods, while its meaning undergoes many changes in line with social development. Benedict, for example, observed that the instability of symbolic meaning is as striking as the stability of seemingly arbitrary ritual acts.[2]

One might speculate whether a changing interpretation of central rituals reflects to some degree the varying development of societies. Initiation into sexual maturity is clearly a central ritual of preliterate society. It seems possible that other rituals which later gave meaning to human life were originally part of it. Of the seven sacraments of the Roman Catholic Church, at least five and possibly six can be recognized as derivatives. Baptism, a ritual rebirth, is one of them. Confirmation in the faith, and possibly Holy Orders, find their counterparts in initiation proper and in the admission to secret religious societies that often follows initiation. Communion, the eating together of food that symbolizes the ritual (if not the god), is another frequent part of initiation. The ordeals imposed on initiates, many of them painful and humbling, may be likened to the sacrament of penance. Thus only two of the seven sacraments are unaccounted for: marriage and extreme unction; and, since initiation among many tribes confers the right to marry, even this is not unrelated. For a time, the process of civilization seems to have run parallel to the separation of a single ritual into constituent parts—and their separation from each other in time.

Such a separation took place among the Kikuyu so recently that it can still be recalled. Among this African people, the rites of marriage and death, which are so important to us, are insignificant compared to initiation.[3] "The symbolic second birth is perhaps the most mysterious of Kikuyu rites. It is one of the oldest customs and universal amongst them, prevailing in all their clans. . . . At one time the new birth was combined with circumcision, and so the ceremony admitted to the privileges and religious rites of the tribe. Afterwards trouble took place . . . the old men settled the matter by separating the two."[4] Too little is said to permit speculation about the psychological reasons for the change or the results of it. As an example it shows how the way was prepared for relegating circumcision to a different, inferior position, a process that has also occurred among the Poro societies of Liberia.[5]

Freud repeatedly made the point that society exacts a heavy price of its members, making them forego pleasures and even accept displeasures in the cause of civilization. Perhaps the reinterpretation of a ritual—from one initially intended to increase pleasure or magic power to one that threatened or banned individual power—perhaps such a change was among the factors creating a type of anxiety that became general in, if not typical of, that society. The anxiety then tended to bring counterphobic elaborations or superstructures—in brief, to help that society along in the process of civilization.

Since these are all speculations, still another may be put forth. Extrapolating from the psychoanolytic theory of human development, one might consider whether, in certain initiation rituals, two different phases of development were not merged—one belonging mainly to the urethral and the other mainly to the phallic phase. Fenichel says that "the pleasure in urinating may have, in both sexes, a phallic and even sadistic significance or it may be felt as 'letting flow,' as a passive giving oneself up and foregoing control. The aim of letting passively flow may be condensed with other passive aims in boys, like being fondled on the penis or being stimulated at the root of the penis."[6] Subincision seems to result in the flow of urine being experienced passively, while the repeated opening of the subincision wound is a massive stimulation of the underside of the body or root of the penis and not of the glans.

Phallic elements, on the other hand, may be seen in the exposure of the glans through circumcision and in the overvaluation of the male part in procreation through the claim that man can give birth. Thus derivatives of two opposing tendencies seem to be merged in one ritual: man's passive role (his desire for feminine satisfactions) and his fixation on the urethral stage of libido development, and his efforts at phallic self-assertion as well (his desire for masculine satisfactions).

The original nature of Jahwe as a fire god, who appeared to Moses in the burning thornbush, fits in with the notion that at the beginning of monotheism, urethral and phallic elements were mixed in a first step toward phallic primacy. This is assuming, of course, that Freud's theory of the origin and symbolic meaning of fire is correct. Technology, characteristic of modern civilization, may have had one of its psychological sources here. Perhaps certain people remained "uncivilized" because they did not feel a psychological need to progress beyond the "passive giving oneself up"; i.e., living more or less dependent on what nature by itself provides. But with phallic psychology aggressive manipulation of nature by means of technological inventions become not only economically useful but psychologically attractive. It should also be noted that the phallic stage, with its aggressiveness (and hence its fear of retaliation), its overevaluation of the penis in particular and of masculinity in general, is accompanied by fear of losing the penis.

In later historic times and in more "civilized" tribes the initiators often use initiation, in part, to exact obedience. But nowhere have I found evidence that further harm to the genitals was among the threats for disobedience. On the contrary, where both circumcision and subincision are practiced, further damage to the penis through subincision is not a punishment but a reward, conferring greater power, greater dignity. Moreover, among the various tribes we can find all the stages of social development.

There are tribes that practice initiation but not circumcision, others in which circumcision is part of initiation but free from any connotations of obedience to elders. Among the most primitive tribes, where subincision is carried to the greatest extreme, there is often the least emphasis on obedience. It may be that even where obedience is demanded, it represents a stage of change from a ritual that began mainly or solely as a means to deal with envy of or anxiety about sex differences, or to gain power over women, or to make possible greater sexual pleasure but then developed into a ritual that lost its original meaning and whose myth is distorted. Such changes from magic efforts to gain power according to the pleasure principle to behavior more consistent with a superego principle would accord with the development of an ever more complex, more id-restricting society.

We might conclude that what was once id-directed is slowly arrogated to the control of the superego—the representative of the elders—before it eventually becomes ego-directed. Circumcision then disappears in Christianity, where the threatening, "castrating" God takes on the additional attributes of a tender, loving Christ. The practise of circumcision is again spreading for supposedly rational, hygienic reasons; but it may also be because sexually we have become a bit freer and hence like to see the glans freed of the foreskin. It might be possible to find among preliterate people, from the aborigines of Australia to more advanced peoples, various stages of initiation rites including circumcision which would show parallel developments. To my knowledge, the search has not been made.

All this has carried us so far into the realm of speculation that one last speculation may be added. In a patriarchal society in which men may have gained ascendance relatively recently, a society which possibly supplanted one in which women had a greater importance, because of their fertility, men may at first go far in asserting their superiority. In reading the Old Testament, there are certain of the Lord's statements to the Israelites asserting His power and uniqueness in which one seems to hear undertones of boastfulness, as if to drown out voices of doubt about all this power, so new. If it were not sacrilegious one would be tempted to say: "Methinks the Lord doth protest too much." Several students of Jewish religion have remarked on this emphatic, defensive, almost querulous assertion to masculine superiority. Sometimes it does not quite succeed in covering the traces of an older cult of maternal deities.

The Jewish myth of the creation seems an example of such defensive overinsistence. Most such myths start with a nonsexual or bisexual god or first man, by or from whom males and females are created at the same time. The Australian aborigines have no such myth as that of a totemic Adam, followed by a totemic Eve as an afterthought; they believe that male and female totemic ancestors existed together from the first.[7] In the Jewish tradition, contrary to the natural course of events, the woman is created from parts of the body of man. Just as an usurper may announce that his right to the throne has existed since time immemorial by claiming descent from an early ruler, so perhaps does the myth project into the beginning of time a dominance only recently acquired. Indeed, myths about the origin of the world or of man are probably projections of conditions either existing or hoped for in the present. Thus the Jewish myth suggests either an actual condition of total male dominance, or the desire for such a condition, while the Australian myth suggests equality of the sexes. This is another reason for doubting that the aborigines now believe in the threat of "castrating" father figures; such a doubt does not apply to the Jews.

Freud seems to have been aware that his speculations about a primal father and his castrating power over his sons did not reach back far enough in time. Perhaps his postulation of an all-powerful father did not reach far enough into the unconscious, either; perhaps his speculations were a defense against the much more omnipotent mother who stands at the beginning of all our lives. Freud admitted his helplessness when confronted with the superior power of mother figures. He said: "I am at a loss to indicate the place of the great maternal deities who perhaps everywhere preceded the paternal deities."[8]

Recently, Roellenbleck approached the problem of Jewish monotheism and its relation to the maternal deities from a psychoanalytic viewpoint. His book refers to many passages of the Old Testament in which, despite seemingly conscious efforts to create a religion dominated by a single, all-powerful god, traces of belief in the maternal goddess are revealed. He discusses, for example, the passage in Exodus in which a woman performs circumcision. Moses' wife Zipporah, after circumcising their son, touches Moses with the foreskin, saying, "Thou art a bloody husband to me." Roellenbleck's interpretation is that, according to early custom, a man becomes suitable for marriage and acceptable to a woman as a husband only by spilling some of his blood from the genital region.[9] Among the ancient Hebrews, as in many modern primitive tribes, initiatory circumcision was a precondition for marriage.

Etymologically, the Hebrew words "circumcisor" and "father-in-law" are so closely related that one can only conclude that once the same term designated both. Nowadays men circumcise boys, and the Old Testament insists that this should be so (despite the story of Zipporah). But this seems to Roellenbleck to be a reversal of the original situation. According to him, it was the initiate who originally had to perform this act of sacrificial mutilation on himself. He thinks that, in a deeper sense, the person who performs the operation is in reality acting merely as a representative of the mother goddess.[10] (*Cf.* the volutary self-castration of the priests of Cybele, pages 91–92.)

Roellenbleck, through his study of the influence of the mother goddess cult on the Old Testament, also came to doubt the validity of some Freudian theories. One of these was Freud's formulation of activity as the man's task in sex, culminating in his penetrating the woman's virginity. Roellenbleck finds instead that "The designation of 'groom' as 'newly circumcised' suggests that the Hebrew male viewed his sexuality primarily not as connected with manly, active powers, at least insofar as he viewed it under a religious frame of reference. Rather, it seems that an unlimited masculine active role was given up in favor of a turn towards passivity."[11]

Whether circumcision was instituted by men or by women, whether it satisfies instinctual desires of men or of women, or both, it can only symbolize castration in a society where severe punishment, particularly in regard to sexual behavior, is part of the individual's frame of reference. And only where the punitive figure of an adult looms large will the child easily make the mental transition from circumcision to castration anxiety. Jewish society is one such, and so are other societies that have been influenced deeply by Judaism.

Zimmerman, too, has recently approached Jewish circumcision from a psychoanalytic viewpoint. He concluded that its significance is less that of symbolic castration than "the wish to create in males a permanent erection of the penis to insure . . . fertile sexuality and thence the continuity of the group."[12] But the idea of, or the wish for a permanent erection seems to belong to the realm of phallic fantasies rather than that of mature genitality. I think that in Zimmerman's, as in certain other psychoanalytic discussions of circumcision, frames of reference, or orbits of experience, seem to be mixed. The circumcised penis can only be experienced as permanently erect by those who have experienced erection. Nunberg's adult patient could feel that circumcision enhanced his (phallic) masculinity; but a "permanent" erection as related to a one-week-old infant has no meaning.

I believe that Zimmerman is correct in relating circumcision to fertility. But it is pubertal circumcision that celebrates the beginning of fertility in the male and not the circumcision of Jewish infants.

Australian Rites

ANTHROPOLOGICAL LITERATURE on initiation is very abundant and a full understanding of puberty ceremonies would demand careful analysis of each part of every ritual. This task I have not attempted. As stated earlier, my purpose was not to solve, once and for all, the ancient riddle posed by initiation and circumcision. I wanted, first, to suggest that Freud's interpretation of these customs is subject to grave doubts, as are the interpretations of those who followed him and saw in ritual circumcision mainly a desire to create castration anxiety. Secondly, I suggested other possible interpretations that I found more in keeping with the facts.

In line with my first purpose, and in justice to Freud, I have relied heavily in this book on the literature he used. My hypotheses must be substantiated or at least not contradicted by his sources; otherwise, because of the great variety of rites, the conclusion would have to be that Freud's interpretations are valid for the tribes he discussed, while other hypotheses may be valid for others. Also, some of the authors who wrote after Freud had formulated his hypotheses (most of them not strictly anthropologists but writers using anthropological data) were so profoundly influenced by him that their interpretations have sometimes derived more from Freud than from empirical evidence—another reason to go back to the sources Freud used.

Freud's anthropological speculations, particularly those on initiation, were based on the writings of Spencer and Gillen (writing of Australia), and of Frazer. But Frazer himself, when discussing Australian aborigines, relied largely on Spencer and Gillen. And indeed, as Freud remarked, these aborigines, like the Australian fauna, have preserved into our our own time much that was archaic and no longer to be found elsewhere.[1] This is especially true of the Arunta who were little influenced by contact with more complex civilizations. They are still considered the most fertile source for investigators trying to understand the spontaneous development, acceptance, and modification of preliterate rites. In 1896, when the Arunta were first studied by Spencer and Gillen, they were almost untouched by Europeans. Their isolated position in the heart of the continent had even kept them from much contact with other tribes and had enabled them to preserve their culture in an unchanged form.[2]

Spencer and Gillen's account of initiation among the Arunta alone covers several hundred pages. These puberty rites comprise the four main phases of (1) throwing the boy in the air and painting him; (2) circumcision; (3) subincision; and (4) the fire ceremony. The first of these is relatively little discussed in the literature and plays no role in the psychoanalytic interpretation of the rites. Perhaps its meaning lies in a first assertion that the boys are going to undergo a major transformation and that the men are going to perform it on them. Perhaps too, these men stand for the mythical first figures with whom the custom originated. The second and third phases of the ritual, circumcision and subincision, have been dealt with at length in the preceding chapters. Therefore, to round out the sequence, an account of the fire ceremony which concludes Arunta initiation is discussed below. So much for Spencer and Gillen on whose reports Freud relied. In addition, I have added a brief account of the Kunapipi, a major cycle of puberty rites in Australia, as reported by more recent observers.

The Fire Ceremony

The fourth stage of initiation among the Arunta and Ilpirra tribes is called the Engwura. It consists of a long sequence of rites, mostly totemistic, lasting for months and terminating in ordeals by fire. Former novices are not fully initiated until this series is completed. All performers in the Engwura are decorated, and the decorations are usually applied to the body by using blood drawn from the subincision wound or from a vein in the arm, as the adhesive agent. The quantity of blood thus used or spilled is enormous, and the ceremonies may lead to total exhaustion of the men who give it. Spencer and Gillen report that one man alone, on one occasion, donated three pints.[3]

Part of the climax of these ceremonies is described as follows:

"After dark a dozen or more fires were lighted. . . .

That night no one in either the men's or the women's camp went to sleep. On the opposite side of the river . . . the light of the women's camp fires could be seen flickering amongst the trees. All night long also the old men kept shouting across to the women, who answered back again, and the scene was one of great excitement. An old man would shout out, 'What are you doing?' and the women would answer, 'We are making a fire.' 'What are you going to do with the fire?' to which the reply would come, 'We are going to burn the men.' . . . In the women's camp all were gathered together at one spot [where they] . . . dug out, each of them, a shallow pit about two yards in diameter, and in each of these, towards daybreak, they made a fire. . . . Then . . . in perfect silence, the whole party [of men] walked in single file [to the other bank]. . . . On the opposite side they halted about fifty yards from the group of women and children who were standing behind the two fires, which were now giving off dense volumes of smoke from the green bushes which had been placed on the red-hot embers. . . . First of all one [sponsoring man] with his [novice] ran forwards, taking a semicircular course from the men towards the women, and then back again. After each of them had done this, then in turn they led their men, running, up to the fires, and one or other of these novices knelt down . . . while the women put their hands on the men's shoulders and pressed them down. In this way the performance was rapidly gone through, not a word being spoken when once the ceremony had begun, each man simply kneeling down in the smoke for at most half a minute. In less than half an hour all was over."[4]

Thus ends the Engwura ceremony, which lasts for many months and requires the most elaborate preparations.

Another of these fire ceremonies is described elsewhere, as follows:

"Avoiding . . . the women's camp . . . the [novices] were taken out through a defile amongst the ranges on the west side of the camp. . . . About five o'clock in the evening all the women and children gathered together on the flat stretch of ground on the east side of the river. . . . A man was posted on the top of a hill overlooking the Engwura ground on the west, and just before sunset he gave the signal that the [novices] were approaching. They

stopped for a short time before coming into camp, at a
spot at which they deposited the game secured, and where
also they decorated themselves with fresh twigs and
leaves . . . Then, forming a dense square, they came out
from the defile amongst the ranges. The [novices] were
driven forwards into the bed of the river, pausing every
now and then as if reluctant to come any further on . . .
After a final pause the [novices] came close up to the
women, the foremost among whom then seized the dry
grass and boughs, and setting fire to them, threw them on
the heads of the men, who had to shield themselves, as
best they could with their boughs. The men with the bull-
roarers were meanwhile running around the [novices] and
the women, whirling them as rapidly as possible. . . .
Suddenly once more the men wheeled around and, followed by [the women], who were now throwing fire more
vigorously than ever, they ran in a body towards the
river. On the edge of the bank the women stopped, turned
round and ran back, shouting as they did so, to their
camp."[5]

The first of these two ceremonies makes it clear that
the women possess power over the fire. They seem to
use it to threaten and dominate the men just as in mythical
accounts, men used to be burned with a fire stick in
circumcision. The men are protected from the threat
(and from the women) so long as they remain separated
from the women by the river. The great hesitation the
men act out before crossing the protective river suggests
once more the magic power that women seem to have
over them. This is demonstrated most vividly by the
women when they press the men down onto the fire, and by
the fact that this act is the climax of the ceremony. The
men's initiation seems concluded when they give up the
protection of the water and submit to the fire and the
women.

After the fire ceremony there seems little doubt that
the novices feel safe with women, who now ritually offer
themselves as sex objects to the men. A last phase of
the ceremonies gives the impression that at the end the
men receive abundant sexual satisfaction.

"When the old men return to their camps and the
[fully initiated men who have just passed through the fire
ceremony] go out into the bush, one or more ordinary

dancing festivals takes place. A special one associated with this period is a women's dance. At night the men and women all assemble in the main camp. . . . As each man approaches the fire he looks about him as if in search of someone, and then, after a short time, sits down amongst the audience. After the men have separately gone through this short performance a number of young women, who have been waiting out of sight of the fire, come near. Each one is decorated with a double horse-shoe-shaped band of white pipeclay which extends across the front of each thigh and the base of the abdomen. A flexible stick is held behind the neck, and one end is grasped by each hand. Standing in a group, the women sway slightly from side to side, quivering the muscles of the thighs and the base of the abdomen in a most remarkable way. The significance of the men's searching looks and of the decoration and movements of the women is evident, and at this period of the ceremonies a general interchange, and also a lending of, women takes place, and visiting natives are provided with temporary wives . . . This woman's dance . . . goes on night after night for perhaps two or three weeks, at the end of which time another dance is commenced."[6]

Fire plays an important part in other initiation rituals besides the Engwura. As various accounts tell us, the earliest method of circumcising was by means of fire sticks which were only later supplanted by stone knives. So it may be that the use of fire and smoke in the final phase of initiation represents a last vestige of circumcision by fire, and of a circumcision or initiation in which women were much more active and dominant throughout.

In a myth of the Wunambal, who live in northwestern Australia, fire itself is said to have originated in subincision. One of their most important mythical ancestors "threw the first flash of lightning by splitting his penis and letting out the fire and the flash of lightning. He created the fire by turning outside the red inside of the split penis till the fire came out."[7]

Fire and urination are also connected with mutilation of the penis in a healing as well as a damaging way. Among some tribes "The blood from the wound is allowed to flow into a wooden shield, which is then emptied into a fire that has previously been prepared for the purpose. If the wound be painful, the initiate puts some glowing pieces of charcoal into the ashes and then urinates upon them, meanwhile holding his penis above the glowing embers, the steam arising in this way from the fire is said to ease the pain."[8]*

The close relation between fire and initiatory circumcision is further corroborated by a comprehensive term used among the Tikopia. This term refers to the firing of the fuel in the cooking place; literally it means "the kindling of the ovens." But the same term covers the whole ceremony of initiation, which includes a slitting of the upper surface of the anterior portion of the prepuce. There is a definite ritual significance attached to this name for initiation.[9]

Fire and Phallic Pleasures

Many have speculated as to whether or not fire was one of the first of man's cultural acquisitions. Was this possession so powerful that its conservation required a central place around which the tribe may have formed? Since fire is usually made by men and not by women, it seems plausible that it was also men who discovered it. Setting and extinguishing fire seem to bring strong phallic pleasures. Whether the preservation of fire was originally entrusted to women is of course highly speculative, particularly since the problem of conserving it seems to have preceded the knack of kindling by some time. But accounts of female fire goddesses whose priestesses were forced to remain virgins suggest that fire had to be protected from men. Other fire gods and goddesses were among the deities served only by priestesses, indicating that perhaps women were responsible for the protection of fire.

Myths such as that of the Wunambal connecting subincision with the acquisition of fire seem to support Freud's notions on the relation between fire and phallic phenomena. He believed that men had to control the wish to extinguish flames by urination, in order to gain permanent possession of fire.[10] And indeed, men who are subincised can no longer direct the stream of urine so well. The pleasure of extinguishing a blaze from a squat-

---

* As noted earlier (page 117), women undergo the same healing and purifying rite after childbirth.

ting position is small when compared with directing a stream of urine at it from a distance.

In view of Freud's speculation, it is interesting that the circumcision damage to the penis, according to Australian tradition, was initially inflicted by fire—an exact reverse of the phallic pleasure of extinguishing flame by urination. If Freud was correct, then the Engwura ritual as well as the Wunambal myth might be interpreted as stating symbolically that men had acquired permanent control of the use of fire.

There are parallels in modern folklore and psychology for the connection between urination and fire. Children are warned not to play with matches lest they wet their beds at night. Fenichel speaks about a deep-seated relationship between urethral eroticism and the excitement aroused by fire.[11] And I have often noticed the delight that boys take in setting fires and in playing with fire pumps, particularly boys in great doubt about their masculinity.

Considering the possibility that forest fires ignited by lightning (see the Wunambal myth) may have been man's original source of fire, the idea of extinguishing it by urination seems ridiculous. But fire caused by lightning may have been preserved in semipermanent small blazes that could easily be extinguished by urination. We have observed how one of our disturbed boys was tempted to urinate at a small fire in an open fireplace, and how the desire was so contagious that all the other boys tried to follow suit. Such collaborative effort could easily douse the small permanent campfire of a tribe.

A number of our enuretic boys have believed that urination was their only protection against destruction by fire. During treatment, they revealed that they drenched their pajamas and bed sheets to save themselves from burning, either by a real fire which they imagined or by the "fire" of their emotions; the danger seemed particularly great to them when they were asleep and so off guard.

Similar unconscious motives might account in part for the fire ceremonies just discussed. Subincised, and thus having symbolically given up the ability to extinguish fire by a stream of urine, the men seek protection behind water, the river. At the end of the ceremony, they experience the women as dangerous and powerful (pressing them down on the fire) but also as benign, since nothing physically harmful occurs and the fire is preserved.

The sequence of the four Arunta puberty rites is perhaps made plainer to the present-day observer if they are read in reverse order (forgetting for the moment the Engwura, which is even more alien to us than the others). While only the most primitive tribes practice subincision, highly cultured nations still circumcise, and the first ceremony, throwing the boy up in the air and then painting him, is like spontaneous adolescent practices known in most modern societies. In this country, it resembles the hazing which, together with final examinations, conferring of degrees, etc., has often been compared with puberty rites. Like many of the rituals devised in prepatriarchal times, these too may have been taken over later by patriarchal society. Then the new system which had to rely on the strictness of its institutions in its early, insecure period, could with growing security relax them.

Looking at the totality of the rituals from this point of view, it is possible to conclude that in the process of civilization—which in many ways parallels the development of patriarchal society—one after another of the initiation ceremonies has disappeared, until only rudiments of the first remain with us. That such a process may have run parallel to a decline in the rigor of the patriarchal system can easily be imagined. As it grew firmly entrenched, it may have depended less on rituals and institutions taken over from prepatriarchal times, and men may have found the need to gain feminine abilities less urgent.

This again is largely speculation. Only the evidence remains: The "ordeal by fire" is the last and perhaps the most profound ceremony, since it signifies not only that initiation is complete, but also, perhaps, the submission of men to women. Immediately before that comes an operation that changes men's anatomy so that they urinate like women and bleed from a genital opening as women do; structurally this operation is far-reaching, but psychologically its effect may be less profound than that of the fire ritual. The still earlier interference with the male genital by circumcision causes it to bleed only once and is even less extensive. Smearing the boys with a substance representing menstrual blood is purely symbolic, while throwing them up in the air is the mildest of all initiation ceremonies.

Viewed in chronological sequence, the rites seem to increase in severity and in making men resemble women, and finally to be dominated by them.

It is impossible to determine—even from a tribe as primitive as the Arunta but at so late a period of their development as the present—whether these rites actually originated with women. But Spencer and Gillen warned against the error, already common in their own day, of speaking as if they were restricted to or belonged only to men; their warning, if heeded by Freud, would have protected him from those speculations connecting the ceremonies with modern castration anxiety. The authors draw attention to tradition after tradition among the Arunta that relate in great detail how, in times past, the things now regarded as taboo to women were not so.*

The authors regard it as unlikely that the aborigines could have invented these details, so contrary to their present ideas, and suggest that the traditions really indicate that formerly men and women were on terms of greater equality than they later came to be.[13] For reasons that we cannot yet understand, ceremonies in which both sexes may have participated were separated into two sets, different in important respects.

The final phase of this presumed development, the only one known to us, shows that for the tribes studied, the male initiation ceremonies are more elaborate than the

---

* Under Ritual Surgery I have cited myths telling of how women originated circumcision. Here I might add the myth, told among the Buka, about the origin of the bull-roarer:

"A woman once went to cut firewood in the bush. . . . She picked up a piece of wood and knocked it on a log. It split in two. One piece flew up into the air and made a noise like this (the teller imitates it). The woman jumped up in a fright: 'What is that?' Then she thought: 'It is something very good. It belongs to me, I found it.' . . . Then she went to her village [and all the women came together and] said 'True, true, you have found a good thing. It belongs to us, you found it.'

"Then all the men came [and wanted to know what all the noise was about. The women told them, and] then all the men went back to their own side of the huts and talked. 'Ah, we had better get this piece of wood, it can cry out.' So the men went and took it away from the women, and they killed . . . them all, except some very tiny girls, hardly more than babies; they were allowed to live because they did not know about the bull-roarer properly."[12]

These and other myths seem to be parallel to those that maintain that circumcision was originally performed by women; they might be viewed as mutually supporting since they are relatively independent of one another.

rites for women, and that women, who formerly played the main role according to legend, are now relegated to a secondary part in ritual life.

Kunapipi

The following brief account of Kunapipi rites is included here because it seemed one of the most characteristic examples of men's preoccupation with female sex functions. Warner has discussed both the myth and the ritual under the name of Gunabibi[14] and more recently Berndt devoted a book-length report to it.[15] These rites occur in areas of Australia where both circumcision and subincision are practiced. The original meaning of Kunapipi is not clear, but it is most frequently translated as "Mother" or "Old Woman." (Used in this context, the term "old" signifies status rather than chronological age.) But "Kunapipi" is also said to have other meanings, including "whistle-cock," meaning a subincision wound, and "uterus of the mother."[16] Even people who practice only circumcision and not subincision use the same name for both subincision and the Kunapipi.

Berndt thinks that the Kunappi cult became merged with that of the Wawilak sisters, and that in this way their myths, which are most directly related to circumcision and subincision (see page 123), became part of the mother-fertility rites.

"This mother is always present behind the ritual, the dancing, and the singing. She is a symbol of the productive qualities of the earth, the eternal replenisher of human, animal, and natural resources; it was from her uterus that human and totemic beings came forth. She has no totem herself, nor is she a totemic concept; she does not herself perform totemic ritual, though her neophytes do. In these areas, she is the background of all totemic ceremony, an 'eternal' explanation and symbol of the Aboriginal way of life, with its continual expectation of rebirth.

"The Mother herself, *Kunapipi, Kalwadi,* or *Kadjari,* is represented in certain parts of the mythology as a perpetually pregnant woman, who in the Dream-Time let out from her uterus human beings, the progenitors of the present natives. She was responsible too for sending out spirits of the natural species from season to season, to

ensure their continual increase. In this she did not act
entirely alone, but in association with a Rainbow Snake,
the symbolic Penis, which completed the dual concept."[17]

Although Berndt calls the snake a penis symbol—
which it also is—in the myths it is most often described
as a female. As a she-snake, it symbolizes the wish of men
for female, (and possibly also the wish of women for
male) sex characteristics and functions.

The Myth

The Kunapipi myth tells how the elder Wawilak sister
gave birth to a child. The sisters then continued their
journey, but the afterbirth blood was still flowing when
they reached the sacred water hole of the mythical snake,
the great Julunggul, who was the "headman" of all animals, birds, and vegetables. The Wawilak sisters made a
fire and placed an opossum on it to roast; but it got
up and ran away, as did all the other animals they tried
to cook. The animals knew that Julunggul was near by,
and that the women were desecrating her water hole by
dropping afterbirth blood around it. The animals disturbed
her by jumping into her well, and she could smell the
afterbirth blood of the elder sister. She lifted her head
from the water, smelling the odor of pollution and sprayed
water upward and outward to form rain clouds.

The two sisters, seeing the clouds, constructed a hut to
protect them from the rain, lit a fire, and went to rest.
The rain began to fall, washing the coagulated blood from
the ground into the sacred well. Julunggul, seeing the
blood in the water, emerged again from her well and
dragged herself toward the bark hut. The Wawilak sisters,
seeing the Julunggul, made attempts to keep her away.

"The younger sister began to dance, to hinder the
Snake's progress. She mover gracefully, shuffling her feet,
swaying her body from side to side. The Julunggul stopped
in her course, and watched the dancing. But the girl grew
tired, and called out: 'Come on, sister, your turn now:
I want to rest.'

"The older sister came from the hut, leaving her child
and began to dance. But her blood, still intermittently flowing, attracted the Snake further; and she moved towards
them.

" 'Come on, sister,' cried the older sister, 'It's no good

for me; my blood is coming out, and the Snake is smelling it and coming closer. It's better for you to go on dancing.' "

So the younger sister continued, and again Julunggul stopped and watched. In this way, the Wawilak danced in turns; when the younger sister danced, the Snake stopped; and when the older one continued, she came forward again. But the younger sister's intensive activity caused her menstruation to begin, and the snake, smelling the menstrual blood and attracted by it, came forward without hesitation. The Wawilak ran into their hut, and, with the baby, sat waiting inside. When Julunggul finally put her head into the hut, she sprayed the women and the child with saliva from her throat to make them very slippery and then swallowed first the baby, then the mother, and finally the younger sister.[18]

Thus it is the female functions involving blood which attract and irritate the great snake; it does not react so to the woman who does not bleed.

As Berndt commented, essentially female sex functions, childbirth and menstruation, are the inciting events in the myth. They arouse the snake, which is powerfully attracted by both menstrual blood and the blood of the afterbirth. The snake puts its head into the hut and spouts forth a slippery substance, a saliva which is called by a word that also designates semen.[19] But why does the snake swallow these three females? (The newborn child is also female.) Perhaps contained in this act lies the explanation for the motives that led to the myth and the rites.

The entering of the snake's head and the spurting forth of the semen-saliva may represent sexual intercourse. But this intercourse is not experienced primarily as an act of procreation, since the aborigines know little of the relation between coitus and conception. Intercourse as described here may be a means of acquiring or being part of the female sex functions. Childbirth took place *before* the snake was attracted; it was the blood resulting from childbirth that initially aroused the snake. When to this was added the attraction of menstruation, the combination became so powerfully stimulating to the snake that coitus took place symbolically. It is, after all, in coitus that the sexes merge most completely, psychologically and physiologically, and a man who wishes to acquire female sex functions might try to do it through intercourse.

But the question of why the snake swallows the three females after coitus is still unanswered. It may be that the victims represent the three main forms in which females and the female sex functions appear to the male: the "sexless" child, the pubertal girl, and the childbearing woman; or the sex functions of menstruation and child-birth. By oral incorporation, the male acquires all three stages of female development as expressed in both cere-mony and myth. If the snake is the symbol of the male organ, it is also the symbol of the incised penis that has taken into itself the incisure, the slit, the vulva, and is thus both male and female. Or as Berndt, concludes, the subincised penis now symbolizes all that is "essential in the process of fructification."[20]

The desire of men to acquire female sex functions in-volves many ambivalences, as does any oral incorporation of a desired and feared object. We should expect therefore to find traditions in which the snake (now both male and female) ejects what it first incorporated. And indeed, the myth tells that later the snake vomits up the women and child, who are then revived. But this is as far as the effort goes toward restoring an unequivocal masculinity. The women are eventually reswallowed.[21]

The Rite

The Kunapipi rite is usually held in the dry season, and the ceremonies last anywhere from two weeks to two months; in exceptional cases they may extend over two years. The rites follow the mythical account closely, though in much abridged form; their sequence of events is also duplicated in the chronological arrangements of the various rites. At the conclusion of the myth the snake, by swallowing the females, has become both male and female. Presumably at the end of the ceremonies the man has done the same by incorporating into himself the fe-male element.

Almost immediately after the first ceremony, the nov-ices, after being smeared with red ochre and blood from the arm, are taken away to meet the Julunggul. As far as the women are officially concerned, the boys are swallowed by the snake, and they are not supposed to return to the society of women until they are reborn at the end of the Kunapipi.[22]*

Warner, in describing what appears to be basically the Kunapipi ceremonies as they occur in Murngin initiation, adds an important element. There, the boys to be circumcised are told " 'The Great Father Snake† smells your foreskin. He is calling for it.' The boys believe this to be literally true and become extremely frightened."[23] Here the scent of the foreskin exercises the same attraction for the snake as did the scent of the blood of the menstruating and childbearing women. Since the foreskin is actually cut off later in the ceremonies, it appears that the snake, which incorporated or wished to incorporate the female sex, now causes bleeding from the male sex organ. If male genital bleeding is not thus made directly comparable to female genital bleeding, it at least seems to represent the satisfaction of a desire aroused by the latter. The Murngin statement reported by Warner continues: " 'This is the blood that snake smelled when he was in the well. . . . When a man has got blood on him [is ceremonially decorated with it], he is all the same as those two old women when they had blood.' "[24]

As the man gives his blood in the ritual, a trumpet is blown over him; this represents Yurlunggur risen from his well to swallow the women because he has smelled the menstrual blood. The songs refer to the profanement of the pool and to the swallowing of the women, meaning that the man who gives his blood for the first time is being swallowed by the snake and is at the moment the mythical woman.[25] When a boy is circumcised it is as if the snake had come again,[26] attracted by the bleeding penis just as in mythical times it was attracted by the bleeding women.

I have interpolated Warner's report here because Berndt does not deal specifically with the connection between circumcision and the Kunapipi and Julunggul rites. But there can be no doubt that circumcision and subincision are directly connected with the myths of the Wawilak sisters, which are also central to Kunapipi.

Berndt does, however, report some of the songs sung

* Thus an element not directly contained in the myth but essential in the acted-out ritual is the connection between initiation and rebirth.

† The "Great Father Snake" is Warner's translation not of Yurlunggur (Murngin for Julunggul) but of another descriptive term sometimes used in addition to Yurlunggur. Yurlunggur is untranslatable.

during the rites which pertain to circumcision and sub-incision. Only key words are sung, and so the author's comments are necessary to understand the meaning of the songs. One of them goes: "Subincised penis incisure [is] open wide," on which Berndt comments: "This . . . refers to [various regions where] the incisure was originally made because of the *Wawilak* (or . . . the *Kunapipi* her-self), in order to represent their vaginae; and the blood coming from the cut (or from subsequent piercing) sym-bolized both the after-birth and menstruation. In the Yirrkalla (northeastern Arnhem Land) version of the *Kunapipi,* the removing of the blood from the arm is a substitute for this practice."[27]

This song and the comments of both Berndt and Warner indicate that blood from the arm, so commonly used in aboriginal ceremonies, is a substitute for blood derived from the genitals, including the subincised penis. This is important because it has been thought that there is a basic difference between "good" blood, coming from the upper parts of the body, and "bad" blood from the lower parts and particularly the genitals.

Another of these songs goes: "Pull foreskin stone knife penis." A translation would be: "Cutting their foreskins with a stone knife." Berndt comments: "The old men see *Buda* and *Bananggala* among the women: they are young boys who have not been circumcised. The [women] say, 'You want to be cut, and then we can copulate better.' Although the two young men were uncircumcised they had been copulating with the [women]; but now the girls persuade them to have their foreskins removed, to make coitus more pleasurable."[28]

The first of these songs thus shows how circumcision and subincision result from events connected with the two mythical women. Men re-enact these events by cutting their penes or their arms to acquire a bleeding, vulvalike opening, and thus to become like the older (childbearing) and younger (menstruating) Wawilak sisters. The second song expresses the belief that it was and is partly due to women's desire that boys are circumcised.

References

Preface

1. M. E. Spiro, [Book review of *Symbolic Wounds*], *American Journal of Sociology* (September 1955), LXI, no. 2, p. 163.
2. *Ibid.*
3. D. F. Aberle, [Book review of *Symbolic Wounds*], *American Sociological Review* (April 1955), XX, no. 2, p. 248.
4. R. Graves, *The White Goddess* (New York: Creative Age Press, 1948).
5. M. Praz, *The Romantic Agony* (Oxford University Press, 1933).
6. D. Riesman, [Book review of *Symbolic Wounds*], *Psychiatry* (1954), XVII, p. 300 ff.
7. E. R. Leach, "Golden Bough or Gilded Twig?" and H. Weisinger, "The Branch that Grew Full Straight," *Daedalus* (Spring 1961), p. 371 ff.

An Ancient Riddle

1. J. G. Frazer, *The Golden Bough* (3rd ed.; London: Macmillan and Co., Ltd., 1922), *Balder the Beautiful*, II, p. 278.
2. M. F. Ashley-Montagu, "Ritual Mutilation Among Primitive Peoples," *Ciba Symposia*, VIII (1946), p. 421.
3. *Ibid.*
4. F. Speiser, "Über Initiationen in Australien und Neu-Guinea," *Verhandlungen der Naturforschenden Gesellschaft in Basel*, XL (1929), pp. 195, 199, 200, 244.
5. B. Spencer and F. J. Gillen, *The Native Tribes of Central Australia* (London: Macmillan & Co., 1899), p. 263.
6. *Ibid.*
7. Speiser, *loc. cit.*, p. 198.
8. N. Miller, *The Child in Primitive Society* (New York: Brentano's, 1928), p. 189.
9. N. Miller, "Initiation," *Encyclopaedia of the Social Sciences* (New York: The Macmillan Co., 1932), VIII, p. 49.
10. B. Malinowski, *Magic, Science and Religion and Other Essays* (Glencoe, Ill.: The Free Press, 1948), p. 21.
11. M. Mead, *Male and Female* (New York: William Morrow & Co., 1949).
12. M. F. Ashley-Montagu, *Coming Into Being Among the*

Australian Aborigines (London: George Routledge & Sons, Ltd., 1937).

13. G. Bateson, *Naven* (Cambridge: Cambridge University Press, 1936).

14. R. M. and C. H. Berndt, *Sexual Behavior in Western Arnhem Land* (New York: Viking Fund Publications in Anthropology, 1951), and R. M. Berndt, *Kunapipi* (Melbourne: F. W. Cheshire, 1951).

15. S. Freud, "Some Psychological Consequences of the Anatomical Distinction Between the Sexes," *Collected Papers* (London: The Hogarth Press, 1950), V, p. 197.

16. S. Freud, *An Outline of Psychoanalysis* (New York: W. W. Norton & Co., 1949), p. 89.

17. S. Freud, "Three Contributions to the Theory of Sex," *The Basic Writings of Sigmund Freud* (New York: The Modern Library, 1938), p. 612.

18. O. Fenichel, *The Psychoanalytic Theory of Neurosis* (New York: W. W. Norton & Co., Inc., 1945), p. 437 ff.

19. E. Neumann, *The Great Mother* (New York: Pantheon Books, Inc., 1955), p. 290.

20. *Ibid.*, p. 159.

Reopening the Case

1. W. Wolff, *The Threshold of the Abnormal* (New York: Hermitage House, 1950), p. 183.

2. T. Reik, *Ritual* (New York: Farrar, Strauss & Co., Inc., 1946), p. 48.

3. L. Rangell, "The Interchangeability of Phallus and Female Genital," *Journal of the American Psychoanalytic Association*, I (1953), p. 504 ff.

4. S. Ferenczi, "An 'Anal Hollow-Penis' in Women," *Further Contributions to the Theory and Technique of Psychoanalysis* (London: Hogarth Press, 1950), p. 317.

5. M. Chadwick, "Die Wurzel der Wissbegierde," *Internationale Zeitschrift für Psychoanalyse*, XI (1925), p. 63.

6. H. Nunberg, *Problems of Bisexuality as Reflected in Circumcision* (London: Imago Publishing Co., Ltd., 1949), p. 22.

7. Fenichel, *op. cit.*, p. 77.

8. Nunberg, *op. cit.*, p. 8.

Challenge to Theory

1. S. Freud, *Moses and Monotheism* (New York: Alfred A. Knopf, 1939), p. 192.

2. S. Freud, *An Autobiographical Study* (New York: W. W. Norton & Co., Inc., 1952), p. 129.

3. S. Freud, *New Introductory Lectures on Psychoanalysis* (New York: W. W. Norton & Co., Inc., 1933), pp. 120–121.

4. Freud, *Outline of Psychoanalysis,* pp. 92–93, footnote 11.

5. Freud, *Moses and Monotheism,* pp. 156–157.

6. E. H. Erikson, *Childhood and Society* (New York: W. W. Norton & Co., Inc., 1950), pp. 82–83.

7. Nunberg, *op. cit.*

8. *Ibid.,* p. 1.

9. *Ibid.,* p. 71.

10. *Ibid.,* p. 63.

11. *Ibid.,* p. 8.

12. *Ibid.,* p. 1.

13. Fenichel, *op. cit.,* p. 364.

14. M. Bonaparte, *The Life and Works of Edgar Allan Poe* (London: Imago Publishing Co., 1949), p. 482.

15. S. Freud, "Totem and Taboo," *Basic Writings,* p. 807.

16. Aberle, *loc. cit.;* and Schneider [Book review of *Symbolic Wounds*], *American Anthropologist,* 57, (1955), pp. 390–392.

17. G. Roheim, *Australian Totemism* (London: George Allen and Unwin, 1925), p. 221.

18. Fenichel, *op. cit.,* p. 450.

19. Freud, "Three Contributions," *Basic Writings,* p. 592.

20. K. Landauer, "Das Menstruationserlebnis des Knaben," *Zeitschrift für Psychoanalytische Pädagogik,* V. (1931), p. 178.

21. M. Chadwick, *loc. cit.,* pp. 61–62.

22. M. Klein, "Early Stages of the Oedipus Conflict," *Contributions to Psycho-Analysis 1921–1945* (London: The Hogarth Press, 1948), pp. 206–207.

23. G. Zilboorg, "Masculine and Feminine, "*Psychiatry,* VII (1944), p. 290.

24. E. Fromm, *The Forgotten Language* (New York: Rinehart & Co., 1951), p. 233.

25. E. Jacobson, "Development of the Wish for a Child in Boys," *The Psychoanalytic Study of the Child* (New York: International Universities Press, 1950), V, p. 142.

26. E. Neumann, *Ursprungsgeschichte des Bewusstseins* (Zürich: Rascher Verlag, 1949).

27. Zilboorg, *loc. cit.,* pp. 275–276.

28. *Ibid.,* p. 288.

29. *Ibid.,* p. 294.

The Blinders of Narcissism

1. S. Freud, *Aus den Anfängen der Psychoanalyse* (London: Imago Publishing Co., 1950), pp. 54–55.

2. *Ibid.*

3. S. Freud, "Charcot," *Collected Papers* (London: The Hogarth Press, 1948), I, p. 12.

4. Nunberg, *op. cit.*

5. F. Schmidl, "Freud's Sociological Thinking," *Bulletin of the Menninger Clinic,* XVI (1952), p. 1 ff.

6. S. Freud, "Analysis of a Phobia in a Five-Year-Old Boy," *Collected Papers,* III, p. 149.

7. Freud, "Some Psychological Consequences," *Collected Papers,* V. p. 188.

8. A. Lommel, "Notes on Sexual Behavior and Initiation, Wunambal Tribe, North-Western Australia," *Oceania,* XX (1949), p. 158.

9. H. Webster, *Primitive Secret Societies* (2nd ed.; New York: The Macmillan Co., 1932), p. 43.

10. Berndt and Berndt, *Sexual Behavior,* p. 16.

11. *Ibid.,* p. 18.

12. *Ibid.,* p. 21.

13. P. M. Kaberry, *Aboriginal Woman, Sacred and Profane* (Philadelphia: The Blakiston Co., 1939), pp. 66–67, 93.

14. Ashley-Montagu, *Coming Into Being,* p. 24.

15. C. G. Jung, *Antwort auf Hiob* (Zürich: Rascher Verlag, 1952).

16. E. Durkheim, *The Elementary Forms of the Religious Life* (Glencoe, Ill.: The Free Press, 1947), p. 224.

17. D. Schneider, *loc. cit.*

18. Schneider, *loc. cit.,* basing his argument on P. Bohannan, "Circumcision among the Tiv," *Man,* 54, (1954), p. 3.

19. Kaberry, *op. cit.,* pp. 81, 164.

20. *Ibid.,* pp. 66–67.

21. Berndt and Berndt, *Sexual Behavior,* p. 15 ff., p. 86 ff.

22. B. Gutmann, *Das Recht der Dschagga* (München: C. H. Beck, 1926), and Berndt and Berndt, *Sexual Behavior.*

23. B. J. F. Laubscher, *Sex, Custom and Psychopathology: A Study of South African Pagan Natives* (London: Routledge & Sons, 1937), p. 113.

24. *Ibid.,* p. 120

25. C. G. Seligman and B. Z. Seligman, *Pagan Tribes of the Nilotic Sudan* (London: George Routledge & Sons, 1932), pp. 518–519.

26. W. L. Warner, *A Black Civilization* (New York: Harper & Brothers, 1937), pp. 452, 453, footnote 3.

27. Seligman and Seligman, *op. cit.,* pp. 518–519.

28. E. M. Loeb, "Tribal Initiations and Secret Societies," *University of California Publications in American Archaeology and Ethnology,* XXV (1929), pp. 249–250.

29. R. Firth, *We, the Tikopia* (London: George Allen and Unwin, Ltd., 1936), p. 466.

30. S. Freud, "The Taboo of Virginity," *Collected Papers,* IV, p. 229.

31. S. Freud, "One of the Difficulties of Psychoanalysis," *Collected Papers,* IV, p. 347 ff.

32. P. Bohannan, "Circumcision among the Tiv," *Man*, 54 (1954), p. 4.

33. Durkheim, *op. cit.*, p. 314.

34. Nunberg, *op. cit.*, p. 22.

35. Durkheim, *op. cit.*, p. 314.

36. M. Merker, *Die Maisai* (Berlin: Dietrich Reimer, 1910), p. 62.

37. F. Bryk, *Neger-Eros* (Berlin: Marcus & Weber, 1928), p. 54.

38. R. Firth, *op. cit.*, pp. 426–428.

39. Bohannan, *loc. cit.*, pp. 2–3.

40. *Ibid.*

Fertility, the Basic Rite

1. R. Briffault, "Fertility Rites," *Encyclopaedia of the Social Sciences*, VI, pp. 190–192.

2. Kaberry, *op. cit.*, p. 203.

3. *Ibid.*

4. M. Raphael, *Prehistoric Cave Paintings* (Washington, D.C.: Pantheon Books, 1945), pp. 5–6.

5. G. R. Levy, *The Gate of Horn* (London: Faber and Faber, 1946), pp. 11–12.

6. R. R. Marett, *The Threshold of Religion* (2nd ed.; London: Methuen & Co., 1914), p. 218.

7. Levy, *op. cit.*, p. 27.

8. *Ibid.*, pp. 36–37.

9. *Ibid.*, p. 53.

10. *Ibid.*, pp. 55–57.

11. *Ibid.*, p. 86.

12. R. J. Braidwood, "From Cave to Village," *Scientific American*, CLXXXVII, 4 (1952), 64, and private communication.

13. C. Strehlow, *Die Aranda und Loritja Stämme in Zentral Australien* (Frankfurt am Main: Joseph Baer & Co., 1910), p. 2.

14. Roheim, *Australian Totemism*, p. 272 ff.

15. H. Nevermann, *Masken und Geheimbünde in Melanesien* (Berlin: Reimar Hobbing, 1933), p. 126.

16. A Krämer, *Die Malanggane von Tombara* (München: Georg Müller, 1925), pp. 60–61.

17. Berndt and Berndt, *Sexual Behavior*, p. 110 ff.

18. *Ibid.*, p. 127.

19. *Ibid.*

Ritual Surgery

1. P. Browe, S.J., *Zur Geschichte der Entmannung* (Breslau: Müller and Seiffert, Breslauer Studien zur historischen Theologie, N.F. 1, 1936), p. 13.

2. *Ibid.*, p. 63 ff.

3. H. W. Roscher, *Lexikon der griechischen und römischen Mythologie*, I, p. 2745.

4. Browe, *op. cit.*, p. 63.

5. W. E. Roth, "An Introductory Study of the Arts, Crafts, and Customs of the Guiana Indians," *38th Annual Report of the Bureau of American Ethnology . . . 1916–1917* (Washington: Government Printing Office, 1924), pp. 417, 591.

6. E. Weigert-Vowinkel, "The Cult and Mythology of the Magna Mater from the Standpoint of Psychoanalysis," *Psychiatry*, I (1938), pp. 348–349.

7. *Ibid.*, p. 352.

8. *Ibid.*, p. 353.

9. *Ibid.*

10. P. P. Chazac, "La Religion des Kikuyu," *Anthropos*, V (1910), p. 317.

11. Spencer and Gillen, *Native Tribes*, p. 251.

12. B. Spencer and F. J. Gillen, *The Northern Tribes of Central Australia* (London: Macmillan & Co., 1904), p. 352.

13. *Ibid.*, p. 368.

14. E. Westermarck, *Ritual and Belief in Morocco* (London: Macmillan and Co., Ltd., 1926), II, p. 427.

15. Fenichel, *op. cit.*, p. 83.

16. G. W. Harley, "Notes on the Poro in Liberia," *Papers of the Peabody Museum of American Archaeology and Ethnology*, XIX (1941), No. 2, p. 15.

17. Firth, *op. cit.*, pp. 446–447.

18. Spencer and Gillen, *Native Tribes*, p. 453.

19. *Ibid.*, p. 454.

20. *Ibid.*, pp. 455–456.

21. B. M. Loeb, "The Blood Sacrifice Complex," *Memoirs of the American Anthropological Association*, No. 30 (1933), p. 18.

22. G. A. Barton, "Semitic Circumcision," *Encyclopaedia of Religion and Ethics* (New York: Charles Scribner's Sons, 1911), III, p. 680.

23. Loeb, *loc. cit.*, p. 21.

24. Warner, *op. cit.*, p. 250.

25. *Ibid.*, p. 512.

26. R. Berndt and C. Berndt, "A Preliminary Report on Field Work in the Ooldea Region," *Oceania*, XIII (1943), p. 257.

27. Ashley-Montagu, "Ritual Mutilation," *loc. cit.*, pp. 432–433.

28. Spencer and Gillen, *Native Tribes . . .* , p. 442.

29. *Ibid.*, pp. 442, 463–464.

30. *Ibid.*, p. 220.

31. *Ibid.*, p. 443.

32. *Ibid.*

33. B. M. Harrison, *Savage Civilization* (New York: Alfred A. Knopf, Inc., 1937), pp. 43–49.

34. Seligman and Seligman, *op. cit.*, p. 518.

35. P. M. Larken, "An Account of the Zande," *Sudan Notes and Records,* IX (1926), p. 1 ff.

36. J. Czekanowski, *Forschungen im Nil-Kongo Zwischengebiet* (Leipzig: Klinkhardt und Biermann, 1924), VI, pt. 2, p. 35.

37. Seligman and Seligman, *op. cit.*, pp. 518–519.

38. Bryk, *op. cit.*, p. 60

39. *Ibid.*, p. 59.

40. Ashley-Montagu, *Coming into Being,* p. 293.

41. Spencer and Gillen, *Native Tribes,* pp. 255–257.

42. *Ibid.*, p. 259.

43. *Ibid.*, p. 93, footnote 1.

44. *Ibid.*, p. 263.

45. W. E. Roth, *Ethnological Studies Among the North-West-Central Queensland Aborigines* (Brisbane: Edmund Gregory, Government Printer, 1897), p. 180.

46. Kaberry, *op. cit.*, p. 43.

47. Spencer and Gillen, *Native Tribes,* p. 263.

48. Warner, *op. cit.*, p. 278.

49. Lommel, *loc. cit.*, p. 159.

50. Roth, *Ethnological Studies,* p. 180.

51. H. I. Hogbin, "Native Culture of Wogeos," *Oceania,* V (1934), p. 330.

52. Webster, *Primitive Secret Societies,* p. 38.

53. R. B. Smyth, *The Aborigines of Victoria* (Melbourne: John Ferres, Government Printer, 1878), I, pp. 60–61.

54. Ashley-Montagu, "Ritual Mutilation," *loc. cit.*, pp. 426, 433.

55. G. Roheim, "The Symbolism of Subincision," *The American Imago,* VI (1949), p. 321.

56. *Ibid.*, p. 324.

57. Ashley-Montagu, "Ritual Mutilation," *loc. cit.*, pp. 432–433.

58. F. Bryk, *Die Beschneidung bei Mann und Weib* (Neubrandenburg: Gustav Feller, 1931), p. 279.

59. G. Roheim, *The Eternal Ones of the Dream* (New York: International Universities Press, 1945), pp. 169–170.

60. *Ibid.*, p. 171.

61. *Ibid.*

62. Ashley-Montagu, *Coming into Being,* p. 301 ff.

63. M. F. Ashley-Montagu, "The Origin of Subincision in Australia," *Oceania,* VIII (1937), p. 207.

64. Spencer and Gillen, *Native Tribes,* p. 464.

65. D. S. Davidson, *The Chronological Aspects of Certain*

Australian Social Institutions as Inferred From Geographical Distribution (Philadelphia: 1928).

The Men-Women

1. R. Briffault, "Birth Customs," *Encyclopaedia of the Social Sciences,* II, p. 566.

2. Sir E. F. Im Thurn, *Among the Indians of Guiana* (London: 1883), p. 218.

3. Briffault, "Birth Customs," *loc. cit.,* pp. 565–566.

4. B. Malinowski, "Culture," *Encyclopaedia of the Social Sciences,* IV, p. 631.

5. Bateson, *op. cit.,* p. 12.

6. W. Eiselen, "Initiation Rites of the Bamasemola," *Annals of the University of Stellenbosch,* X (1932), p. 17.

7. Frazer, *op. cit., Adonis, Attis, Osiris,* II, p. 263.

8. O. F. Raum, *Chaga Childhood* (London: Oxford University Press, 1940), p. 309.

9. Frazer, *op. cit., Adonis, Attis, Osiris,* II, p. 264.

10. A. C. Hollis, *The Nandi: Their Language and Folk-Lore* (Oxford: The Clarendon Press, 1909), p. 58.

11. E. Crawley, *The Mystic Rose* (New York: Boni & Liveright, 1927), II, p. 24.

12. Frazer, *op. cit., Balder the Beautiful,* II, pp. 249–250.

13. *Ibid.,* p. 251.

14. Harley, *loc. cit.,* p. 15.

15. G. Schwab, "Tribes of the Liberian Hinterland," *Papers of the Peabody Museum of American Archaeology and Ethnology,* XXXI (1947), p. 284.

16. Harley, *loc. cit.,* p. 17.

17. K. Abraham, *Selected Papers* (London: The Hogarth Press, 1949), p. 463.

18. Frazer, *op. cit., The Magic Art,* I, pp. 96–97.

19. Frazer, *op. cit., Balder the Beautiful,* II, p. 248.

20. Hollis, *op. cit.,* p. 56.

21. Warner, *op. cit.,* pp. 267, 328.

22. Bateson, *op. cit.,* p. 77.

23. Mead, *op. cit.,* p. 67.

24. *Ibid.,* p. 98.

25. Miller, "Initiation," *loc. cit.,* p. 49.

26. Crawley, *op. cit.,* II, p. 3.

27. Laubscher, *op. cit.,* pp. 113, 123, 130.

28. Gutmann, *op. cit.,* p. 317 ff.

29. R. H. Lowie, "Age Societies," *Encyclopaedia of the Social Sciences,* I, p. 482.

30. H. Blüher, *Die Rolle der Erotik in der Männlichen Gesellschaft* (Jena: E. Diederichs, 1921), II, p. 91 ff.

31. Spencer and Gillen, *Native Tribes,* p. 274 ff.

32. *Ibid.*, p. 272.
33. Harley, *loc. cit.*, p. 3.

The Secret of Men

1. Kaberry, *op. cit.*, p. 241.
2. *Ibid.*, pp. 244–245.
3. Berndt, *Kunapipi*, p. 8.
4. *Ibid.*
5. *Ibid.*, p. 55.
6. *Ibid.*, p. 58.
7. Harley, *loc. cit.*, p. 14.
8. R. H. Lowie, *Primitive Society* (New York: Boni and Liveright, 1920), pp. 265–266.
9. B. Blackwood, *Both Sides of Buka Passage* (New York: Oxford University Press, 1935), p. 244.
10. *Ibid.*, p. 245.
11. *Ibid.*, p. 194.
12. *Ibid.*, pp. 194–195.
13. Raum, *op. cit.*, p. 355.
14. *Ibid.*, pp. 318–319.
15. Gutmann, *op. cit.*, p. 325.
16. Roheim, *The Eternal Ones*, p. 171.
17. Raum, *op. cit.*, p. 350 ff.
18. Gutmann, *op. cit.*, pp. 364–365.
19. *Ibid.*, p. 325.
20. Briffault, *loc. cit.*, p. 192.
21. J. Henry and Z. Henry, *Doll Play of Pilagá Indian Children* (New York: American Orthopsychiatric Association, Inc., 1944), p. 10.

Girls' Rites

1. Raum, *op. cit.*, pp. 349–350.
2. G. W. K. Mahlobo and E. J. Krige, "Transition from Childhood to Adulthood Amongst the Zulus," *Bantu Studies*, VIII (1934), p. 166.
3. Mead, *op. cit.*, p. 175.
4. C. M. N. White, "Conservatism and Modern Adaptation in Luvale Female Puberty Ritual," *Africa*, XXIII (1953), p. 15 ff.
5. L. Mair, "A Yao Girl's Initiation," *Man*, LI (1951), p. 60.
6. Spencer and Gillen, *Native Tribes*, pp. 459–460.
7. *Ibid.*, pp. 460–461.
8. *Ibid.*, p. 461.
9. B. Spencer and F. J. Gillen, *The Arunta*, (London: Macmillan and Co., Ltd., 1927), I, p. 222.
10. F. McKim, *San Blas: An Account of the Cuna Indians*

of Panama (Goteborg: Etnologiska Studier, XV, 1947), pp. 79–84.

11. Freud, "The Taboo of Virginity," *Collected Papers,* IV, pp. 221, 231.

12. Freud, "Totem and Taboo," *Basic Writings,* p. 831.

13. *Ibid.,* p. 847.

14. R. Benedict, *Patterns of Culture* (Boston: Houghton Mifflin Co., 1934), pp. 28–29.

15. G. Devereux, "The Psychology of Feminine Genital Bleeding," *The International Journal of Psycho-Analysis,* XXXI (1950), p. 252.

16. *Ibid.,* p. 252, footnote 19.

17. *Ibid.,* pp. 252–253.

18. Roth, *Ethnological Studies,* p. 174.

19. *Ibid.,* pp. 177–178.

20. Berndt, *Kunapipi,* p. 67.

21. J. Mathew, *Eaglehawk and Crow* (London: D. Nutt, 1899), p. 121.

22. Kaberry, *op. cit.,* p. 99.

23. Bryk, *Neger-Eros,* p. 56.

24. M. Bonaparte, "Notes on Excision," *Psychoanalysis and the Social Sciences* (New York: International Universities Press, 1950), II, p. 79.

25. *Ibid.,* pp. 81–82.

26. Bryk, *Neger–Eros,* p. 55.

27. M. J. Herskovits, *Dahomey* (New York: J. J. Augustin, 1938), I, p. 282.

28. White, *loc. cit.,* p. 20.

29. M. J. Herskovits, *Dahomey,* p. 278.

30. Bryk, *Neger–Eros,* p. 34.

31. M. Bonaparte, "Notes on Excision," *loc. cit.,* p. 81.

The Biological Antithesis

1. A. Werner, *The Natives of British Central Africa* (London: Constable & Co., 1906), pp. 126–127.

2. M. Van Waters, "The Adolescent Girl Among Primitive Peoples," *The Journal of Religious Psychology,* VI (1913), pp. 375–421, VII (1914), pp. 75–120.

3. C. G. Jung, "Psychic Conflicts in a Child," *The Development of Personality* (New York: Pantheon Books, 1954), p. 5.

Appendix: Infant Circumcision

1. C. C. Sherman, "Circumcision," in S. M. Jackson, ed., *The New Schaff-Herzog Encyclopedia of Religious Knowledge* (New York: Funk and Wagnalls Co., 1909), III, pp. 117–119.

2. R. Benedict, "Rituals," *Encyclopaedia of the Social Sciences*, XIII, p. 397.

3. W. S. Routledge and K. Routledge, *With a Prehistoric People* (London: Edward Arnold, 1910), p. 154.

4. *Ibid.*, p. 151.

5. Harley, "Notes on the Poro," p. 15.

6. Fenichel, *op. cit.*, p. 69.

7. Kaberry, *op. cit.*, p. 198.

8. Freud, "Totem and Taboo," *Basic Writings*, p. 921.

9. E. Roellenbleck, *Magna Mater im alten Testament* (Darmstadt: Classen & Roether, 1949), p. 71 ff.

10. *Ibid.*, p. 74.

11. *Ibid.*, pp. 71–72.

12. F. Zimmerman, "Origin and Significance of the Jewish Rite of Circumcision," *The Psychoanalytic Review*, XXXVIII (1951), p. 112.

Appendix: Australian Rites

1. Freud, "Totem and Taboo," *Basic Writings*, p. 807.

2. Ashley-Montagu, *Coming into Being*, p. 14.

3. Spencer and Gillen, *Native Tribes*, pp. 370–372.

4. *Ibid.*, pp. 374–380.

5. Spencer and Gillen, *The Arunta*, I, p. 278 ff.

6. *Ibid.*, I, pp. 297–299.

7. Lommel, *loc. cit.*, p. 160.

8. Ashley-Montagu, "Ritual Mutilation," *loc. cit.*, p. 428.

9. Firth, *op. cit.*, pp. 423–424.

10. S. Freud, "The Acquisition of Power Over Fire," *Collected Papers*, V, p. 288.

11. Fenichel, *op. cit.*, p. 371.

12. B. Blackwood, *op. cit.*, pp. 216–217.

13. Spencer and Gillen, *Native Tribes*, p. 457.

14. Warner, *op. cit.*, p. 290 ff.

15. Berndt, *Kunapipi*.

16. *Ibid.*, p. 16.

17. *Ibid.*, p. 13.

18. *Ibid.*, pp. 20–23.

19. *Ibid.*, p. 25.

20. *Ibid.*

21. *Ibid.*, p. 31.

22. *Ibid.*, pp. 41.

23. Warner, *op. cit.*, p. 261.

24. *Ibid.*, p. 278.

25. *Ibid.*

26. *Ibid.*, p. 287.

27. Berndt, *Kunapipi*, p. 110

28. *Ibid.*, p. 168.

INDEX